Remember When

Celebrating the history of Washington and Greene counties in Pennsylvania.

Presented by the

Observer-Reporter

Contents

Foreword

On an August afternoon in 1808, two itinerant printers – William Sample and William B. Brown – rolled into the village of Washington on a Conestoga wagon, loaded with tools of their trade: a hand-operated press, paper and ink. Bound for the very edge of the frontier – then in Kentucky – they were instead persuaded by an innkeeper to stay here and set up shop in his cellar.

The newspaper they began printing was *The Reporter*. Little could they imagine that nearly 200 years later their little enterprise would not only still exist but be the predominant source of information – every day – for an area of more than 250,000 inhabitants.

It is with great pride that we at the *Observer-Reporter* look back upon the history we have chronicled. And it is with this book that celebrates the history of Washington and Greene counties that we launch our own bicentennial celebration.

The 21 chapters of "Remember When" were first published over three years in the pages of the *Observer-Reporter*. The articles were highly popular with our readers, who each year seem to demand more and more content of historical interest. Many of these articles required months of painstaking research and much cooperation from our readers, who provided us with valuable information and photos.

The articles were the work of writers and editors under the direction of staff writer Terri T. Johnson, who leads the *Remember When* special project team. We must also acknowledge the assistance of others, particularly Beverly Fox, photography department secretary, who retrieved many of the photographs in the book from our archives: Canonsburg historian Dr. James Herron, who provided photos for several of the stories; the Washington County Historical Society; the Greene County Historical Museum, and Audrey Huffman.

Neither this book nor the *Observer-Reporter* would exist without the support of our loyal readers and subscribers, and it is to them that we dedicate this work.

A. Parker Burroughs
Editor

'Auld' Land Syne

September 26, 2004
A tragic fire in 1963 consumed Washington's Auld Hotel

By Christie Campbell

On Christmas morning 1963, the Auld Hotel in downtown Washington was destroyed by fire, killing one of its guests.

Soon after, the building would be razed, ending the existence of a hotel on the site for 145 years.

For travelers of the National Pike, the Auld Hotel on the northwest corner of Main and Maiden streets was a welcome stop for the night. For locals, its dining rooms and bar served as a gathering place for casual get-togethers as well as special events.

"They had the best pecan pie in the world," said Katherine Vaughn, who frequented the hotel's restaurant. Vaughn, corporate secretary to Ben Richman for 50 years (he was the last owner of the hotel), remembers being awakened that Christmas morning by a telephone call alerting her that the hotel was on fire.

The Washington Observer reported that 14 guests were able to get out of the hotel, with the exception of 53-year-old Earl E. Yaugher of Baltimore.

Yaugher was found dead on the second floor, the same floor where the fire was believed to have started when an unidentified guest fell asleep smoking a cigarette.

Jack Manning, former fire chief for the city, remembers that firefighters found about half a dozen spent fire extinguishers near the fire's origin. Apparently attempts were made to put out the fire before the fire department was called.

"If they had called us right away, we could've put it out," Manning said.

The damage was so bad that the original building had to be razed. But its northern addition, which now houses a Pennsylvania Liquor Store, remains. Upstairs, the hardwood floors of the hotel's old ballroom remain, along with evidence of a fire there 40 years ago.

Chris Potts, one of the partners in Auld Hotel Properties, which owns the whole city block, has plans to turn the ballroom into four studio apartments.

The hotel's history began when James Ashbrook conveyed the lot to Daniel Moore in 1812. Moore, an early settler of Washington, was a stage line owner. He erected a three-story building on the corner. No mention is made of the hotel's name, although in May 1821, Samuel Dennison advertised his Travelers Inn and Stage Office at the site.

In 1823 James Briceland took over the hotel and named it the National House. Two years later James Dunlap became owner,

Left: The Hotel Auld as it appeared at the northwest corner of Main and Maiden Streets in the 1930s.

calling it the Jackson Hotel, for Gen. Andrew Jackson, who stayed there the night of March 21, 1825.

The property would later change hands numerous times: to John Irens, James Searight, Daniel Valentine, George Hammond, Edward Lane and Adam Morrow. It was then called the Rail Road House, but one photograph shows it painted with The Morrow House in large letters on the side of the building.

Then, in 1880, James Auld purchased the hotel and the name stuck, though it had numerous owners afterwards. When Auld acquired it, he enlarged the building by adding a fourth story and erecting the three-story addition on its north side.

According to the Industrial Edition of the Washington Weekly Democrat published in December 1897, the Auld House was operated by I.H. Taylor.

Rooms were available for $2 a night and featured "airy, well-appointed sleeping rooms and a cozy parlor and sitting room."

A dining room that seated 75 people was on the ground floor with 45 sleeping rooms upstairs.

The hotel boasted fire escapes, electric bells and gas heaters in the rooms.

"A splendid, well-provisioned table is kept. The service is prompt and courteous, everything possible is done to promote the comfort of the guests," the newspaper account reads.

Adjacent was Robert Price's barber shop that featured six barber chairs.

"The interior fittings and appurtenances of

Above: Spectators view the fire damage to the Auld Hotel on the morning of December 26, 1963. The State Store at right was saved and still operates today.

Right: The Auld House—with a new fourth floor and an addition on the north side—was decorated for Washington County's centennial celebration September 7 and 8, 1881. A large evergreen arch was erected in front of the building for the festivities.

Far Right: The hotel at the northwest corner of Main and Maiden streets changed hands many times from 1820 to 1880, when James Auld purchased it. This photo is from the late 1860s, when Adam Morrow owned it.

Right: On December 25, 1963, the Auld Hotel, at the corner of Main and Maiden streets in downtown Washington, was destroyed by fire, killing one guest. A hotel had existed on that site for 145 years.

this tonsorial parlor are unsurpassed in the locality and no expense or pains have been spared here in marking this as an attractive an establishment as one would seek to find," the flowery newspaper account read.

A native of Lexington, Va., Price worked in Canonsburg. He later sold Price's Hair Restorative from the business.

In 1890 the Bigger and Bingham hardware store was in the front portion of the building, but another photograph shows the Sharp Brothers business in the same window. Brooms and rain barrels are for sale in front of the store.

Photographs of the building show it decorated for the city's centennial celebration in 1881. One photograph shows an arch over Main Street with the Auld House in the background. According to an article written by historian Harriet Branton, the archway, festooned with evergreens, was one of three erected over Main Street for the centennial.

People who remember dining at the Auld Hotel recall the detailed woodwork. Some portions were saved. Bill Montgomery, of Duncan Avenue, managed to save eight oak beams as the building was being demolished.

Montgomery, who served as the city's building and housing inspector, installed one beam in his home as a fireplace mantel.

Also salvaged from the building were two stained-glass windows, one of George Washington and the other of Thomas Jefferson. Today, the two windows are in the Rossin Student Center of Washington & Jefferson College. They were donated to the college by Ben Richman.

Above & Left: A fireman is shown on the fire escape of the Auld Hotel during the blaze that charred guest rooms.

Staying Power

Published September 25, 2005
Meadow Lands social club the last remaining den of
Fraternal Order of Bears.

By Michael Bradwell

When the Bears Club was rearranging things in the 67-year-old den after doing some remodeling in the early 1990s, someone started to take down a framed photo of President Franklin D. Roosevelt that had hung on the walls since the 1930s.

Members who were present that day immediately protested, saying the portrait should stay put. Today, Roosevelt continues to look across the room at the members seated at the bar at the Meadow Lands club.

Not only has the local den survived America's lengthy prohibition from alcohol, it also survived a temporary name change, a fire that destroyed an earlier meeting place as well as an attempt to wrest it from its immigrant roots.

When Den 83 of the Fraternal Order of Bears formed in Meadow Lands in 1913, it was seven years before the passage of the 1920 National Prohibition Act, also known as the Volstead Act.

No one knew it then, but the local den would be the only Bears Club in the country to survive America's 13-year social experiment with Prohibition, which Roosevelt ended in 1933.

The local club was formed at a time when fraternal organizations of every stripe were springing up all over the United States. Like other fraternal societies, the Bears is a secret lodge that collects dues, has a password, ceremonies and initiation rites. But on a recent late-afternoon visit, the bar scene at the Bears Club could have been repeated anywhere in Southwestern Pennsylvania - a midweek, after-work group of about 20 people sitting on stools, drinking beer and quietly talking or watching television.

Don Zofchak, police chief of South Strabane Township and a 32-year member of the den, said the lodge, which today has a membership of around 500, continues to be a gathering place for many area residents.

"Prohibition and the Depression killed the other lodges," Zofchak said, recalling walking down a street in Johnstown several years ago and looking up to see a Bears Club sign over the entrance to a building as the last vestige of a den that had been located there.

According to a social history of the Meadow Lands club compiled by Mary Ann Bazzoli in the mid-1970s, the original Bears Club formed 92 years ago, at a time when Meadow Lands was a bustling mining community that was called "Ewing Station"

Left: Bears Den 83 in Meadow Lands.

by Pennsylvania Railroad workers and was on the streetcar line operated by the Pittsburgh Railroad Co. that ran between Pittsburgh and Washington. Bazzoli, of Chartiers Township, wrote the paper as part of a college course that studied the needs a fraternal club addressed in contemporary society.

In the early days, the local club was a social hub for many working men in the Meadow Lands area.

"In that day, people didn't travel a lot, so it was like a Meadow Lands gathering place," Zofchak said of the early days of the club. "It was a neighborhood thing."

The Bears Club actually has its roots as a meeting place in a Meadow Lands miners' hall in 1911, where men of various ethnic backgrounds could relax and have a drink after working long days in the mines. The meeting place was organized by George Fenton Sr., a boss in the Richill Mine; Nick Bellino, the beer distributor of Zelt's Brewery, and Squire Joseph Robinson.

At the time of its charter, the ethnic mix of the club was skewed to those of Anglo-Saxon backgrounds, judging from the names on the charter: George Ford, Bill Edwards, Joe Moore, George Fenton Sr., George Fenton Jr., Joseph Robinson, Isaac Fenton, Bill Haviland, Dominic Bilhive, Bob Finney, Bill Chanute and Bill Whitehouse. A field organizer from the Grand Den of the Fraternal Order of Bears at Columbus, Ohio, presented the men with the charter on Jan. 15, 1913.

As Bazzoli noted in her study of the club, the booming local mines were drawing many immigrant workers, who had left their families in Europe until they could earn enough to pay for their passage to America. As families reunited here, the Bears Club became a social hall that encouraged family attendance and sponsored weekly dances.

While a man would never take his wife into a local saloon, he would take her and the children to the private tables in the back room of the club.

With growing numbers of Italians, Slovenians and Poles as members, it was common to hear foreign languages spoken in the club.

With its long hours and its designation as a social center for miners and their families, the Bears Club thrived. In addition, it offered members sick benefits and funeral benefits in the days when their employers provided only wages.

Bazzoli, who wrote the paper in 1974 for an American Studies course at California University of Pennsylvania and now teaches prisoners at SCI Greene in Waynesburg, said studying the organization showed her how vital it was for men who were new to this country.

"If they didn't help each other, they weren't going to make it in this country," Bazzoli said last week. "It was their glue."

The biggest challenge came in 1920, when the National Prohibition Act was passed, forbidding the production, sale and use of alcoholic beverages.

The act's passage forced the club to take a new name - the Beacon Club - as well as a new charter. Club officers began producing their own moonshine and home-brewed beers in the club's basement, and business was conducted as usual until a U.S. marshal padlocked the establishment for violation of the Volstead Act.

Another local organization, the Allison Athletic Club, leased the building until the repeal of the Prohibition Act. The sports-minded Allison Club's membership rose from 25 to more than 100 members, with most of the new recruits coming from the ranks of the Bears. While the Allison Club maintained prohibition in the hall, Bazzoli's research found that beer-drinking was common among those who accompanied the club's softball, baseball and soccer teams when they played other area clubs. There also were professional fights held on the second floor of the club.

In 1933, Joseph Moore, a Den 83 officer and

Above: Fraternal Order of Bears Den No. 83 logo

a grand officer of the Columbus headquarters, informed the local den that Prohibition and a general lack of interest were responsible for dissolving the other national dens. The Meadow Lands den voted to reopen the Bears Club and became the grand den.

On Oct. 10, 1937, a fire destroyed the building, but members were determined to continue it. Until 1939, when the present two-story brick building was completed on the original site on Hallam Street, members rented a vacant store on Pike Street for their activities.

In 1945, when the club hosted a reunion for members who served in the armed forces during World War II, the Bears had continued their tradition as a social club while putting new emphasis on athletic events in the community, a carryover from when it was reorganized after Prohibition was repealed.

Over the ensuing years, club members participated in dartball and bowling leagues, while others have been active in supporting Little League baseball teams in the area. In addition to its traditional blue-collar membership, the club has attracted its share of professionals and celebrities, including pop singer and recording artist Perry Como, two-time World Lightweight Boxing Champ Sammy Angott and harness horseracing great Delvin Miller. For years, the club sponsored the annual "Old Timers Reunion," honoring men from various states representing athletic interests in golf, boxing, horse racing, football and baseball.

While members still gather to shoot pool, play cards or watch sporting events on television, the club also continues to include activities for couples and families. It also supports area community groups and functions.

"The Bears have survived, and we're more than holding our own," Zofchak said. Of the 500 memberships, he said about 250 of them are active.

Unlike the earlier times, when most members tended to come from the mines around Meadow Lands, today's membership is more diverse, coming from Washington, Canonsburg and throughout Chartiers Township.

Den 83 continues its charter as a grand den - and the only one that remains out of a total that may have numbered in the hundreds before Prohibition.

A number of years ago, Zofchak said, the local club was contacted by a group in Atlanta, Ga., requesting information about obtaining a Bears Club charter.

"We sent them the information, but we never heard anything back," he said. "I don't know what we would have done if they had asked for a charter."

Above: Members of Fraternal Order of Bears Den 83 who served in World War II were treated to a reunion upon returning home in 1945. The Meadow Lands social club is the last remaning den of Fraternal Order of Bears.

Now boarding...
the Blue Ridge Bus Lines

Published May 21, 2006

By Byron Smialek

Back in the day, well before fast food and high-priced gasoline, you could get just about anywhere you wanted to go by bus.

The saying, "You can't get there from here," didn't apply: If you could get to a main road where a regularly scheduled bus ran, the driver would stop and pick you up.

In Washington and Greene counties in the '30s, '40s and '50s, before the advent of the family car, a Blue Ridge Lines bus was the way to go.

"For anybody who wanted to ride a bus, all they had to do was put out their hand and we'd stop and pick them up," said Bill Orndoff, 80, one of the few remaining Blue Ridge bus drivers.

"That's what we did as drivers. We'd pick up customers wherever they were along our route. Of course, there aren't many buses anymore, and they don't make unscheduled stops," he added. "Bus companies are all about staying on schedule. We were all about picking up passengers and still managed to stay on schedule."

Alex Hamilton, a farmer and life-long resident of Brush Run Road in Hopewell Township, northwest of Washington, recalled how his grandfather, Alexander Hamilton, would begin his journey to Washington by hitching a horse to a buggy and driving it the two miles to the intersection of present-day Route 844 (back then Route 31) and Brush Run Road.

"He'd tie up the horse at the Red Barn there and wait for the Blue Ridge bus to come along and take him the rest of the way into Washington," Hamilton said.

"My grandfather would do whatever business he had to do that day in Washington, and then catch the bus back to the Red Barn to get his horse and buggy and drive it home," he said. "That was back in the '30s, as I recall, maybe even the early '40s during World War II and gas rationing."

His grandfather never drove a car.

"You know those buses would stop anywhere you were along the road," Hamilton added. "As a kid, I lived on a farm down the hill from Buffalo Village on the main road, and the driver would stop there and take us to town and drop us off there on the way back.

"Either that, or we'd hitchhike," he said. "You wouldn't want to do something like that nowadays. Hitchhiking wouldn't be a safe thing to do today."

Left: Passengers wait to board a Blue Ridge Lines bus bound for Pittsburgh.

In the Beginning

In the years before World War I, one of the earliest public utility holding companies, the Hagerstown & Frederick Railway, was formed to include local street railway and electric power companies in both of those Maryland cities, plus an interurban trolley line that connected those cities to a smaller railway and power system in Pennsylvania, as well in northern Virginia.

In 1923, a group of Cumberland, Md., businessmen, backed by Baltimore-based Potomac Public Service, formed Blue Ridge Transportation Co., and for $110,000 purchased an early but extensive bus operation that linked Hagerstown with Cumberland to the west, Winchester to the south, Smithsburg to the east and Baltimore (via Frederick) in the southwest.

Westward expansion began in October 1927 with the purchase of Old Trails Bus Line and service between Frostburg, Md., and Uniontown. Four months later, a logical extension from Uniontown to Pittsburgh completed the 235-mile main line between Baltimore and Pittsburgh that had four round trips per day, mostly following the National Road (today's U.S. Route 40).

A Sept. 29, 1929, timetable shows the completed Uniontown-to-Pittsburgh link followed a route through Brownsville to Charleroi, Monongahela, Finleyville and Castle Shannon. That route planted the seed of what was to become the latter-day Route 88 Transit System in the Mon Valley.

In 1931, all bus services operated by companies and subsidiaries owned by West Penn Electric (forerunner of today's Allegheny Power Co.), which

Right: One of the streamlined Blue Ridge Buses.

Above: Just before the company sold out to Greyhound, Blue Ridge buses looked like this.

itself had acquired Potomac Electric and other interests, began to use the trade name of "Blue Ridge Lines."

Those big, distinctive blue and white Blue Ridge/White Star buses were outfitted as motor

Above: Wilbur "Mac" Murray drove for Blue Ridge Bus Lines in its heyday.

coaches with comfortable reclining seats for the long haul from Steubenville and Wheeling to Pittsburgh and back. Even in later years, when some carriers cut back on the long routes and concentrated on local city services, buses through Washington to Pittsburgh were mostly motor coaches.

"I went to work for the Washington city bus company right after World War II and joined Blue Ridge later, about 1948 or 1949," said Orndoff, who is best known in the Washington area as a longtime South Strabane Township supervisor and South Strabane Volunteer Fire Department chief.

"I really enjoyed driving buses," he said. "You got to know the people who rode your bus every day. They'd tell you that they weren't going to ride the bus the next day for some reason, that way we wouldn't look for them."

A New Company Emerges

After the federal government ordered the break-up of electric conglomerates in the mid-1950s, including its ties to the trolley and bus industries, West Penn Power divested itself of Blue Ridge/White Star lines, which, in 1955, were acquired for a time by Greyhound Lines.

Greyhound, in turn, decided to get out of the short-hop bus business when it became more profitable to make big city runs using the just-developing interstate highway system.

"To tell the truth, what Blue Ridge had, Greyhound killed," Orndoff said.

Then along came its successor, Suburban Bus Lines.

"That started out as big joke," he confessed. "That's when I asked the guy from Greyhound that if instead of eliminating the Washington service, the old Blue Ridge Lines routes, I said, 'Why don't you sell it to us drivers?'

"I wasn't really serious about it when I piped up. I mean, I hadn't even given serious thought to where money for something like that would come from, but two weeks later I got a call from Greyhound management about arranging a possible sale."

Orndoff and a dozen others, including, as he remembers it, two other Blue Ridge employees, driver Ray "Sam" Kirschner and mechanic/maintenance man Charles Minor, invested "something like $3,000 each" and became owners of Suburban Bus Lines, which lasted here until 1982.

The roll of charter investors, along with Orndoff, Kirschner and Minor, included Jack Tarr, a bus ticket agent from Canonsburg, J.C. Hilty, Carl Wilson, Frank Liberatti, Rich Gregg, Harold Gregg, Joe Lorenetti, Frank Olczak and Coen Oil Co. and Guttman Oil Co.

Tarr became the first president of Suburban Bus Lines, followed by Orndoff and then J.C. Hilty, who became the third and last president of Suburban Lines. Shortway Bus Co. from Toledo, Ohio, bought out Suburban interests in 1982, and operated local bus service to Pittsburgh as Shortway-Suburban until 1985, when it disappeared entirely.

"You might not know this, but at one time, Suburban Bus Lines was in The Wall Street Journal," Orndoff said. "We got a big write-up. That's when we had about 100 employees and we were making 44 round-trips a day into Pittsburgh.

"But what killed us was when Interstate 79 opened," said Orndoff, who, although now 80, still works as a part-time courtesy car driver for Washington Ford. "Before the interstates came along, our buses would always be packed with riders.

"Everybody had cars by then, and it was more convenient and also more private for couples, boyfriends and girlfriends, in particular, to go to Pittsburgh together in a car than by getting on a bus," Orndoff added.

This writer and his brothers and sisters had a personal connection with Blue Ridge Lines. Growing up in downtown Cecil in the 1950s, the four oldest Smialek children delivered the two afternoon Pittsburgh daily newspapers back then, The Press and the Sun-Telegraph.

Bundles of those two newspapers came out of Pittsburgh on a Blue Ridge bus headed for Steubenville, Ohio, via a route from Bridgeville to Avella, to Wellsburg, W.Va., to Steubenville.

The bus driver always carried the wire-bundled papers off his bus and deposited them on the concrete porch stoop in front of our house.

"Yep, that's what we did back then," said Orndoff, who provided the name of Bill Cook as

the fondly remembered driver who delivered the bundles of papers that we delivered faithfully every afternoon for years. "That sounds like something that Cookie would do."

Sources: Ed Lybarger, volunteer archivist and events manager and now bus specialist, at Pennsylvania Trolley Museum, Arden; Jack E. Syphers of Wheeling, W.Va., Suburban Lines retiree, who spent more than 30 years as a scheduler for Consolidated Bus Lines; American Motor Bus Society, Bill Orndoff, J.C. Hilty, Alex Hamilton and Carol Claffey Mounts.

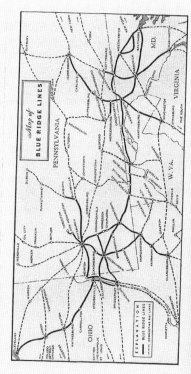

Above: A Blue Ridge Lines buses brochure from the 1950s.

Born From Coke and Smoke

Published June 13, 2004
Donora was a boomtown fueled by the industrial revolution.

By Scott Beveridge

Land speculators camped overnight beside stakes marking vacant lots in Donora before a property auction began at 10:30 a.m. Sept. 10, 1901.

"A gun was fired and the rush for lots started," local historian J.P. Clark wrote in a 1951 story about the rise of this gritty mill town.

Within a day, 200 lots sold for more than $100,000 near mills that would become infamous for the smoky air they produced.

The land sale was announced after Richard B. Mellon purchased 230 riverfront acres for the Union Improvement Co. of Pittsburgh. He and his brother, Andrew, also had a friend in Fayette County, coke baron Henry Clay Frick, who was investing with them in this once-picturesque curve in the Monongahela River valley known for its thick air.

Riverboat captains had long called this stretch of the river Hell's Bottoms because of their limited view during foggy weather.

William H. Donner was the first entrepreneur to be drawn here as the nation's Industrial Revolution was exploding. Donner, who was born in 1864 in Columbus, became president of Union Steel Co. in 1899, three years after building a tin mill in nearby Monessen.

Donner was attracted to the area because of its proximity to the region's rich coal and natural gas deposits. He opted, however, to sell his Monessen business to American Tin Plate Co. and concentrate on Donora.

In 1898, Donner wanted to compete against American Steel & Wire Co. of New Jersey. That company was forming a monopoly in steel, threatening the interests of Carnegie Steel Co., which included Frick among its largest suppliers. Industrialist Andrew Carnegie saw no other way to compete against American Steel & Wire unless he built blast furnaces in Donora to supply Donner's new mills.

The creation of Union Steel was announced June 21, 1901, in the local weekly newspaper, The Donora American, at about the time the giant U.S. Steel Corp. was formed.

The Donora headline forecast the creation of one of the largest independent steel plants in the country, at a cost of $20 million. This new company boasted it soon would employ 10,000 workers. The partnership also was building the largest rod, wire and nail mills in the world, plants that would be operating within a month in Donora. The same day, Donner announced his $1

Left: A cinder ladle for pouring molten steel is on display at an open house at the mill circa 1950.

million purchase of the Mesaba Iron Ore Range in Minnesota. It was the largest iron region in the world, and its mineral reserves would provide the source for manufacturing iron ore in Donora for years. The borough also incorporated that year, taking its name from Donner and Nora Mellon, wife of A.W. Mellon.

The "wheels were turning in the rod mill" for the first time at noon Aug. 9, 1901. "Almost every one of the local officials has lost a suit of clothes or two or wages as to the starting of the works," the Donora newspaper reported.

The new mills outpaced projections that they would produce a million kegs of nails, and 200,000 tons each of rods and wire within a year. Donner and Frick further proved themselves industrial powers when Union Steel absorbed Sharon Steel Corp. in November 1902. Union Steel now had the capacity to produce 850,000 tons of steel, controlling 6,000

acres of coal reserves in the region. A month later, U.S. Steel reacted by purchasing Union Steel for $45 million, solidifying the world's then-largest manufacturing corporation.

The Donora mills became known as American Steel & Wire, a division that by this time had become a subsidiary of U.S. Steel.

Prior to 1900, Donora was known as the West Columbia section of Carroll Township and home to just a handful of farm families. By August 1902, there were 5,082 people living in the crowded town. Newcomers eager for jobs faced severe housing shortages.

The first billets of steel were produced in another expansion three years later at Margaret Furnace, one of two, new $2 million blast furnaces.

Immigrants needed to be strong to survive Donora. Many of them worked the equivalent of a second job building a family home after toiling long

hours in the mills, according to modern scientist and environmental author Devra Davis. A typical laborer dug his home's basement and lined its floor with concrete, and his family lived in the foundation until it could afford additional floors, the Donora native stated in her 2002 book on air pollution, "When Smoke Ran Like Water."

The room-and-board problem became a housing famine by 1915, when U.S. Steel announced it was building a $3 million zinc plant at the northern end of town. Local health officials were concerned about the spread of disease with as many as three families and boarders sharing cramped quarters.

The zinc mill was the largest and most modern such plant in the world, employing 2,100 workers. By 1920, steel men were quitting their jobs because they could not find homes. The borough's population soon swelled to its peak of 15,000.

Work was especially tough in the zinc mill.

Above: A panoramic view of the former American Steel & Wire Co. from a Webster hillside after the turn of the 20th century.

Born From Coke and Smoke

While laborers then spent between eight and 12 hours a day in the steel plant, zinc workers could withstand only three hours a day working beside the smelters. The temperature there hovered at 120 degrees. "It was really back-breaking work in intolerable heat," Davis said, speaking in Donora in April. In addition to zinc, the plant produced alloys strong enough to make U.S. Army tanks bulletproof.

It wasn't the strength of U.S. Steel or its laborers that put Donora on the map, however. The borough captured national news when 20 people died, some gasping for air, within a few days while a heavy fog settled over the valley, beginning on Oct. 26, 1948. Seventeen of the deaths occurred within 12 hours, while thousands were sickened or fled to the countryside. Five days later, a mill attorney ordered the cooling of the zinc smelters as mill chemists began arriving in Donora. Investigators with the Pennsylvania Department of Health also came to

town that day. Many local residents blamed the deadly air on the zinc mill, which spewed sulfurous fumes, carbon monoxide and carbon dioxide, along with various heavy metal dusts.

The downwind residents of the village of Webster, Westmoreland County, reacted by forming one of the first anti-pollution groups in the nation.

The society criticized U.S. Steel for its strong influence over the Donora Borough Council, which ignored its pleas for a local clean air ordinance. United Steelworkers of America Local 1758 representatives held six of the seven seats on council at the time.

Residents of Donora and Webster sued American Steel & Wire in federal court in the late 1940s and early 1950s, hoping to expose the zinc mill as the source of the foul air. In all, 132 lawsuits were filed over the smog. The corporation reached $500 settlements with some of the plaintiffs, without

admitting responsibility for damages, court records indicate. A U.S. Public Health Service investigation found no single cause for the smog, placing much of the blame on an unusual weather pattern that trapped the air in the valley.

Federal lawmakers, however, noted the damage to Webster and the smog deaths in support of enacting the nation's first anti-pollution legislation in 1963, and the Clean Air Act of 1970.

Some Donora residents attempted to erase the smog from the borough's history. Clark, the historian, did not mention the nation's worst air pollution disaster in his story in the Donora Jubilee, a local magazine that celebrated the borough's golden anniversary. The company stated its "sincere hope" in the magazine that it would be around and flourishing for another 50 years.

"The Donora Steel and Wire Works is proud of its production achievement, especially during

the war years when all facilities were utilized for producing war materials," the company proclaimed in a pamphlet distributed during a 1948 open house. The plants had the capacity to produce 476,000 tons of hot-rolled rods a year, along with 260,000 tons of bright wire annually. "More coal is consumed in the mill in one month than what is required for heating 1,700 average family residences for a year."

U.S. Steel's 1951 vow of continued prosperity in Donora was short-lived. In 1957, the company permanently closed the zinc mill, citing depleted ore reserves and outdated equipment as reasons for its demise.

Donner's early promise of creating 10,000 jobs in Donora never materialized, either. Employment peaked after the zinc mill opened at nearly 7,000. For their remaining history, the mills employed between 3,000 and 5,000 workers, depending on the economy.

This same mill and town shared a radical and sometimes violent history. As early as 1902, Donora police were being stationed at Slavic weddings because shootings often took place at the receptions. Borough officials were launching crusades against gambling houses as early as March 1905. Forty percent of the men in Donora gave the World War I draft board fictitious addresses in protest.

During the first steel strike in 1919, dynamite was used to set off explosions at the homes of two men who crossed the picket lines. No one was injured, but the windows were shattered. Early in the labor dispute, a mob of angry strikers disarmed the local police chief, hitting him about the face, as the burgess was escorting the mill superintendent through the zinc works gate. These striking workers were encouraged to use violence during an Oct. 7, 1919, meeting in nearby Charleroi with Mary Harris "Mother" Jones, a politically charged, elderly labor organizer.

For days during Mother Jones' visit, the borough was marked by labor riots. On Oct. 9, 1919, the wives of striking workers participated in a riot that included gunfire. A different mob of 50 men carrying bricks and stones attacked three black men seeking work. The staff at the local district justice's office was overworked because so many laborers were being arrested in this unsuccessful strike for an

Above: In a circa 1950 photograph of service award presentations at the Donora blooming mill are, from left, G.D. Johnston, Michael Kalko, Andrew Fedor, Donald Guarascio, John Daugherty, James Godwin, Charles Gee, Charles Fritch and Michael Opatkiewicz.

eight-hour workday.

The entire work force in Donora walked off the job in a 1936 strike one year before the United Steelworkers of America was recognized as its union.

U.S. Steel's operations were affected by outside labor problems, as well. The remaining mills were closed for a week in June 1957. The layoffs took place during a strike called by 5,100 workers on Donora Southern Railroad, which supplied the mills with raw materials and hauled its finished products. During this strike, the railroad workers prevented U.S. Steel from upgrading the mills by blocking new equipment from being delivered by rail. The company chose to reroute the train to improve a steel plant in Cuyahoga, Pa.

On June 24, 1962, U.S. Steel confirmed the permanent closing of Donora's steel mill. The company was cleaning house due to obsolete operations, a declining market for wire and competition from West Germany.

The Donora rod and electric weld shops operated, sporadically, through 1967, when U.S. Steel finally abandoned Donora after investing heavily in mills in Gary, Ind., and Fairless Hills, Pa. Most of the remaining mill buildings were quickly razed, and the property donated to the Washington County Redevelopment Authority.

Donora's downtown and neighborhoods spiraled into a steady decline because of lost real estate and wage taxes. The population dwindled to 5,693 when the 2000 census was taken.

Today, a century-old, soot-stained metal warehouse beside the Donora-Webster Bridge is among a few reminders that a mighty and historic mill once stood along the river.

Left: Thompson Avenue in Donora, as it appears today.

Lost Landmark

Published July 18, 2004
Early Canonsburg amusement park struggled
with mishaps and bad luck.

By Michael Bradwell

For nearly a decade, from the late 1920s through the mid-1930s, motorists driving in South Strabane Township along Route 19 from Canonsburg to Washington could see The Brown Flyer rising above them, a half-mile-long roller coaster that served as the beacon to Mapleview Park.

But Mapleview's big wooden coaster, like the park itself, seemed doomed to a short, difficult run. Early access problems, the death of two customers, a riot and other financial challenges exacerbated by the Great Depression made it impossible for Mapleview to achieve the longevity of Kennywood or Conneaut Lake Park, despite its attempts to remake itself.

But for a brief time, Mapleview, located just behind what is today Auggie's Road House along Route 19, was a magnet for those who wanted to while away a summer's day riding the rides,

---

Left: Mapleview Park was an early Canonsburg amusement center that operated from the late 1920s through the mid-1930s. Early access problems, the deaths of two customers, a riot and other financial challenges exacerbated by the Great Depression made it impossible for the park to achief the longevity of Kennywood.

playing skill games or dancing to big band music far into the night.

An Inauspicious Start

In January 1927, a company called Maple View Recreation announced plans to build an amusement park on a 100-acre farm owned by R.G. "Bert" Lutton, a former Washington County sheriff, on Hill Church Road between Washington and Canonsburg. Lutton was the owner of the attraction, backed by several investors.

Mapleview Park opened to the public on Memorial Day 1928, boasting the Ritz ballroom that could hold 3,500 people and included a restaurant dining room and picnic area; a large merry-go-round; a swing ride; the half-mile-long Brown Flyer roller coaster, and promises of other amusements to be ready by July 4, including a swimming pool.

The additional amusements were added, but the pool would never be built.

The first in a series of mishaps at Mapleview happened less than a month after its opening. On June 29, 1928, Samuel Malone, 22, of Burgettstown, was killed instantly after he fell from the Brown Flyer.

Following a jury trial in Washington County Court, Malone's mother, Annie Malone, was awarded $10,435 on March 14, 1930. Defense attorneys attempted to prove the roller coaster was not dangerous, introducing expert testimony that no safety devices were needed on the cars when passengers held onto metal bars inside the cars. Malone's death was ruled accidental.

The park continued to operate, but just a year later, on July 7, 1929, Mario Mark, 15, of Canonsburg, was killed when he was thrown from the coaster. Several eyewitnesses said Mark was not wearing a safety belt and had been standing up, despite warnings for him to sit down.

Less than a month before the park was ordered to pay Malone's mother, a trial began on Feb. 25, 1930, with Tony and Gaetano Mark bringing suit against Mapleview for their son's death. Eyewitnesses

Above: An aerial view of Mapleview Park during its operation.

recanted earlier accounts that Marks had been standing in the coaster. Mapleview's management was found negligent in the case, and was ordered to pay the Marks $1,000.

Hopes for Profit

In March 1930, Mapleview was placed in receivership. While the company continued to do business, principals said business was down considerably because of the closing of Hill Church Road, but hoped to be operating profitably in the summer of 1930.

A spring 1930 article in the former Daily Notes reported that Mapleview was expecting "the biggest season since the company was organized," and Lutton sounded excited, predicting that the principals expected to earn a profit and planned to continue enlarging the park.

Lutton was hopeful that the swimming pool would be built that year, adding that water had been provided for all of the buildings. The park also had its own power station, which generated electricity for the rides and lit up the midway.

It looked as though 1930 would be Mapleview's breakthrough year. Before it opened, it was reported that at least 75 area organizations had booked dates at the park. The operators announced the arrival of a manager for the ballroom, which was enlarged and redecorated and appeared to be a major part of a strategy for turning a profit.

Sara Carothers Bougher, 85, of Dormont, a niece of Lutton, remembered visiting her

uncle's amusement park as a girl, recalling the merry-go-round, the Brown Flyer and other rides. As a teenager, she said, she and some of her friends would occasionally visit the big dance pavilion, which was along Route 19.

Mapleview's newspaper ads throughout the early '30s describe dance contests at the ballroom that appeared to be similar to the marathons popular during the era, inviting guests to compete for local, state and national championships. An August 1934 ad offered prizes, mentioning that national winners would receive stage contracts and a free movie tryout.

The music was live, provided by big bands from Pittsburgh and others that were known nationally. One of the biggest bands to play Mapleview in 1930 was "McKinney's Cotton Pickers," which made numerous records and radio appearances in the late 1920s and early '30s. The McKinney band was led by Don Redman - who would later lead and record swing bands under his own name in the 1930s - and also included others who would go on to greater fame, including saxophonists Benny Carter and Coleman Hawkins and pianist Fats Waller.

Big Band Echoes

Jim McBride now lives in Cleveland but remembers hearing the strains of music coming from Mapleview's bandstand on summer evenings when he was a teenager staying at his family's farm on McBride Road, which was adjacent to the park.

"On a clear night, you could not only see the outline of the park, but you could hear the music," McBride recalled.

As a young teenage ticket-taker at the merry-go-round ride in the first two seasons of Mapleview, Mike Dayak of Muse recalled big crowds on the midway, but said many more people turned out for the big-band music.

"You could hear the echo of the music up to a mile away," Dayak said, recalling big bands led by Fred Waring and Guy Lombardo playing at Mapleview whenever they passed through the area.

The bands started playing around 9 p.m. and went until 1 a.m. It was the era of Prohibition, but Dayak said that didn't stop some of the patrons from taking a drink.

"Some of them would bring moonshine," he said, adding that Mapleview's parking lot often would be littered with empty bottles on mornings after a dance.

For 1935, the park underwent another name change. A large newspaper ad in June of that year announced the grand summer opening of Club Mapleview, "The Dance Spot Beautiful." The "All-Star Revue" slated for June 21, 1935, included Shirley Heller, a radio singer; several dancing acts, and music provided by "The 10 California Cadets." Patrons paid a cover charge of 25 cents for an evening of music and dancing.

But two months later, on a mid-August evening, a large crowd grew ugly when employees decided to stage an 11 p.m. strike and demand back pay they said was due them for the prior two weeks.

According to news stories from the time, the two bands slated to play that evening also demanded their pay, and when it wasn't forthcoming, withdrew from the bandstand. Around midnight, about 200 couples began demanding table service and music, with some tearing off table and chair coverings in protest. An on-duty constable was unable to control the crowd, and state police were called to help quell the uprising.

Louis Frishman, who was manager of Club Mapleview, was attacked during the riot, and later would face a dozen charges, including his failure to pay semi-monthly wages twice in August.

In October 1935, the Brown Flyer was dismantled by workmen, its lumber sold off. The loss of Mapleview's big wooden landmark was a harbinger of its impending demise.

Just over a year later, on Dec. 1, 1936, Club Mapleview itself disappeared forever, a victim of a fire that destroyed the large, wooden recreation center that also included a three-room dwelling in the rear.

Not long before the fire, the property had been sold to J.B. Goldberg of Sharon and was under lease to Louis Weiner, who had managed the club since May 1936.

While Goldberg had carried insurance on the property, there was no coverage on the restaurant equipment, bar or other fixtures in the building, all of which were destroyed.

Staff writer Sarah E. Core provided research for this story, gathered from the files of Dr. Jim Herron of Canonsburg.

Above: A 1930s newspaper ad announces dancing at Mapleview Park's ballroom.

Left: Mike Dayak, 85, of Muse, a caretaker at Chartiers Hill Presbyterian Cemetery, was in his early teens when he worked as a ticket-taker at Mapleview's merry-go-round. Dayak said Mapleview's live big-band music was as big of a draw as its rides and skill games.

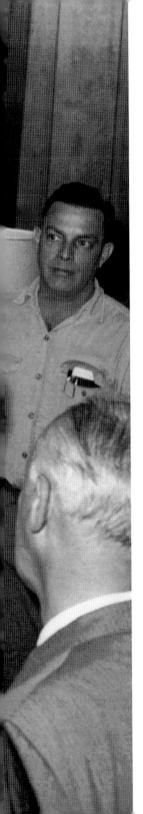

The JFK Mystique

Published April 23, 2006

By Brad Hundt

It's the hair that Cary Jones remembers.

As a 9-year-old, he watched John F. Kennedy sweep up Beau Street seated on the trunk of a convertible, and what still stands out is the color of the 35th president's hair.

"It wasn't as red as I thought it would be," said Jones, who is now 53 and an attorney in Washington. "It was more brown. We had a black and white TV, and to see a person like that in true, living color was really something.

"He was the first famous person I'd ever seen," Jones recalled.

Forty-two years after Kennedy's death, the "thousand days" of his presidency still exert an unshakable fascination. The stream of books on Kennedy continues unabated, especially around landmark anniversaries of his assassination, and, in a 2003 Gallup poll, he came in second in the "greatest presidents" tally, bested only by Abraham Lincoln.

During one of the thousand days of Camelot, Kennedy broke away from Washington, D.C., and visited Washington, Pa.

On Oct. 13, 1962, Kennedy came to the city on a campaign

Left: Doris Stiltenpole, then an employee of the George Washington Hotel, hovers behind President Kennedy and his entourage as they arrive October 13, 1962.

swing a little less than a month before that year's midterm election. It was at the tail-end of a two-day journey through the Pittsburgh area that included a rally at the University of Pittsburgh and visits to Aliquippa, McKeesport and Monessen.

While Kennedy was ostensibly stumping for fellow Democrats, he was undoubtedly thinking ahead to his own re-election prospects in 1964. In the nail-biting 1960 election, Kennedy carried Pennsylvania with 51 percent of the vote over Richard Nixon's 48 percent. And, much like Al Gore in 2000 and John Kerry in 2004, Kennedy ended up carrying Pennsylvania on the strength of victories in the Philadelphia and Pittsburgh regions. Kennedy carried Washington County by 15,000 votes and Greene County by 2,000 votes, and also took Allegheny, Beaver, Fayette and Westmoreland counties.

"We're here for the Democratic Party," Kennedy told the crowd, which clogged the street in front of the Washington County Courthouse and spilled onto Beau Street that Saturday afternoon.

The opportunity to engage in a little partisan hardball before friendly crowds might have been a welcome respite from the troubles bedeviling Kennedy in the Oval Office.

Just two weeks before, James Meredith became the first black student at the University of Mississippi after federal intervention; and the Cold War relationship between the United States and the Soviet Union was about to turn positively glacial. The day after

---

Kennedy's visit to Washington, a reconnaissance flight over Cuba revealed Soviet missiles being installed, kicking off the two-week-long Cuban Missile Crisis.

It was the first time a sitting president visited Washington since Benjamin Harrison came for a funeral in 1892. It hasn't happened again in the four decades since, though Bill Clinton made a stop at Washington's Union Grill restaurant prior to Pennsylvania's Democratic primary in 1992.

Preparations for Kennedy's Washington appearance were completed close to the time Air Force One touched down at Greater Pittsburgh Airport. Workmen constructed a platform outside the Main Street entrance to the courthouse, and a sign that read "WELCOME MR. PRESIDENT" was hung between two courthouse pillars.

Parking was prohibited on portions of Beau and Main streets and on all of Cherry Avenue. The courthouse was shut down and additional phone lines were installed to accommodate the press traveling with the president.

The weather that day? "Perfect," according to The New York Times.

Despite the golden glow that now surrounds the Kennedy legend, not everyone was enthusiastic about his presence in Washington. Some protesters held up signs at the rally, with one proclaiming "JOBS, NOT JIBES," and another that said nothing more than "TALK, TALK, TALK, TALK, TALK."

The Observer, which was seldom shy about its

Above: The car in which President Kennedy is riding stops at the entrance to the George Washington Hotel October 13, 1962. Seated next to Kennedy is Richardson Dilworth, former mayor of Philadelphia, and Pittsburgh Mayor David L. Lawrence.

Right: A huge crowd turned out to see President Kennedy on October 13, 1962. It turned out to be the day before the start of the Cuban Missile Crisis.

The JFK Mystique

Republican leanings in those days, offered lukewarm editorial support the day before Kennedy's arrival. "Many of those who hear him will be persons who are greatly opposed to his political theories and to his record in office," the newspaper opined, "but it is to be expected that all of them will respect the office to which he was elected two years ago … Respect does not necessarily mean agreement."

The Pittsburgh Press was even less kind: "We'd feel a lot safer if JFK would stick to his job and let his political friends do their own campaigning."

Nevertheless, "there was quite a bit of buzz about it," according to Jack Crouse, who covered Kennedy's visit for the Observer and The Washington Reporter. "He was a popular figure, certainly, and a charismatic figure.

"I can picture the crowd in front of the courthouse," he continued.

Before being called away to fight a house fire, retired Washington fire Chief Jack Manning saw Kennedy's motorcade pull in behind the courthouse.

"He was a handsome man," Manning recalls. "That's unusual for a man to say, but he was a striking individual. He was tanned, like he'd just been to Florida."

Malcolm Morgan, who would one day be a Washington County commissioner, was working for York Realty at the time, and watched the rally from his sixth-floor office in the Washington Trust Building, which faces the courthouse.

Above: President Kennedy greets people outside the Washington County Courthouse.

Above: Well-wishers greet President Kennedy as he arrives in Washington October 13, 1962.

Left: "We're here for the Democratic Party," President Kennedy told the crowd in front of the Washington County Courthouse during his visit.

Morganza

Published March 27, 2005
Reform school was the traditional penalty handed down to the
youthful troublemakers of bygone days.

By Brant M. Newman

The biggest threat one can hold over the heads of misbehaving children in the 21st century might be the loss of Internet privileges, but a half-century ago in Western Pennsylvania, parents could - and did - trot out a much scarier threat: accommodations at Morganza.

The name, itself, suggests a pastoral wonderland where a boy could spend his days skipping stones on a pond and fishing in the old mill stream. It was pastoral; there was no doubting that. It's unlikely, however, that the young miscreants - both girls and boys - who were sent there to be straightened out thought of it as resort living.

Local historian Dr. James T. Herron Jr., whose father was the veterinarian for the animals on the Morganza farm, grew up among a generation of children who knew what fate awaited them if they deviated from the straight and narrow.

Left: Cadets from Morganza, a reform school opened in the 1870s on the former Morgan Farm march on Harrison Street in Canonsburg for a 1902 centennial celebration. More recently, Morganza was the site of Western Center.

"Kids were always told, 'You behave yourself, or you're going to go to Morganza.' It was used an awful lot," Herron said.

Morganza, more recently the site of Western Center, the state facility for the mentally retarded, was rolling farmland when the state decided in the early 1870s that its Pennsylvania Reform School in Pittsburgh needed a more bucolic setting. Hence, acreage that once was the home of the Morgan family was purchased and turned into a setting where "bad kids" could be restored to the paths of righteousness.

Boys and girls from across Pennsylvania and from other states were committed to the reform school. According to an 1892 report by officers of the school, the young offenders ranged from the simply incorrigible to those who had been guilty of vice and crime but were not yet "hardened in sin" and appeared capable of being reformed.

The aim of the school, according to the report, was to change the children into good citizens through a combination of "wholesome restraints, moral influence and formation of industrious habits."

If idle hands are the devil's workshop, the young inmates at the reform school held little interest for the red guy with the pitchfork.

Classroom work took up 6 1/2 hours a day. The rest of the time was spent learning trades and performing work necessary to

---

Above: Girls at Morganza learned about the domestic sciences, including cooking and laundry.

the operation of the youth center.

In the early days, there was a shoe shop, tailor's shop, a stable for the farm's draft horses, a kitchen for preparing meals and a full-scale working farm complete with dairy cows, hogs, sheep and chickens. Other trades taught to the boys included carpentry, painting, printing and bricklaying.

The girls at Morganza were restricted in the early years of the school to the "domestic sciences": cooking, laundry, mending and the like.

But Herron squashes any notion that the girls of Morganza fit into the category of the "fairer sex."

"They were considered more dangerous. I taught Sunday school at Morganza, and supposedly the girls were harder to control. They were more sullen. The boys were more talkative," he said.

Herron recalls the time when a boy from Philadelphia asked him in Sunday school about the "methods of castigation" in the Bible.

"A girl in the class replied, 'I don't think they did that to them,'" Herron said, noting that the girl apparently confused castigation with a rather delicate medical (or anger-related) procedure.

The Morganza school had first through 11th grades and was accredited by the state. In 1930, the average age of admission was 15 for boys, 16 for girls, but one boy was only 7 and one girl 9.

The sexes were almost totally segregated, seeing one another only in chapel or at special events such as the big July 4th parade and celebration held at the school for many years. The school, itself, had very little interaction with the surrounding populace, save for performances by the Morganza marching band in Canonsburg parades.

For the best-behaved youngsters, freedom might be won after 20 months at Morganza, but the norm was two years, and those released before adulthood stayed under state parole until age 21.

Mary Alice Norcik of Heidelberg spent two years at Morganza as a child, but not as an inmate.

Before World War II, when Norcik was in first and second grades, her father, Paul Davis, was in charge of the farming and horticulture programs at the school.

The family lived in a big farmhouse on the Morganza property, and Norcik's mother sometimes was called upon to help the boys at the school can vegetables grown on the farm.

"She said they were all very nice, very polite with her," Norcik recalled.

Norcik's memories of the time spent at the

Above: Boys stand at their desks while doing schoolwork at Morganza.

Above: Girls work the farm at Morganza, a reform school opened in the 1870s on the former Morgan Farm.

Below: Boys work in the shoe shop.

reform school include playing with her younger brother in the creek that ran from the dam on the Morganza property, where many local residents would go to fish. She also attended Muse Elementary School, which entailed a daily walk of 1.2 miles each way, a fact that no doubt was impressed upon her own children.

Norcik also recalls a trip to the "mansion," the still-standing administration building that later served Western Center.

"My parents were friends with somebody who lived in the mansion. ... He was the superintendent, I guess. As a little girl, I remember going to that mansion and going up in the elevator."

If Norcik was concerned about living among "inmates," she doesn't

remember it, except for one incident that has stuck with her through the years.

"I can remember once my father calling home and telling my mother to lock all the doors and windows because a boy had escaped," she said. "I remember my mom was frightened but tried not to frighten us."

The boy was quickly captured and caused no harm.

Norcik's stay at Morganza ended when World War II began and her father entered the military.

Years later, she would make trips back to see her old home.

"I drove through just to see where the house had been, and for the longest time it was still standing," she said. "But when Southpointe came in, it came down."

Morganza still was operating full-tilt in the 1950s, with more than 80 buildings on 1,200 acres. There were 235 boys living in eight large "cottages" and 135 girls housed in six buildings.

But, eventually, the state decided it was cruel to force the inmates to labor on the farm and in the shops, and that was the beginning of the end of Morganza.

After several years of co-existing on the property with the new Western State School and Hospital for the retarded, the last inmate left Morganza in 1967, and kids in Western Pennsylvania could breathe a little easier.

Sources: Dr. James T. Herron Jr. and Jefferson College Historical Society

Above: Superintendent W. Frank Penn (Center, first row) poses with his staff at a time when Morganza operated as a military school.

Right: An overview of Morganza.

Below: Girls wear sashes bearing names of states during a July 4th celebration at Morganza.

'Patch'...
A Great Place To Grow Up

Published April 24, 2005
Philadelphia Place: A 'model community' ahead of its time.

By Byron Smialek

At one time scores of coal mines dotted the region, and with them came row upon row of company-owned houses to be occupied by mine employees.

Many of those so-called "company towns" have survived into the 21st century. More, however, have vanished into history or quickly fading memory.

One such company town now consigned to faded photographs and yellowing newspaper clippings was Philadelphia Place in Canonsburg. It vanished from the landscape more than 30 years ago without so much as a trace.

The area started out as New Philadelphia in the late 1890s, taking its name from the long-forgotten Philadelphia Gas Co. pumping and pressurizing station built near the railroad tracks that paralleled Adams Avenue at the crossing of College Street that extended to the old Weavertown Bridge.

Big, old, wooden-sided, two-family homes with small yards,

Left: Many of the houses of the former Philadelphia Place, or "Philly Patch," had already been razed to make way for the Chartiers Creek Flood Control Project by the time this photo was taken in the mid-1960s. By early 1973, the last of the houses had been demolished.

board fences, clothing hanging out to dry in the breeze, dusty and narrow streets were built for the men who mined the coal and their families.

The name New Philadelphia never really caught on, becoming Philadelphia Place, and then, somewhat derogatorily, "Philly Patch." Those who hung that name on it did not take into account the soul of the place and the high regard in which it was held by its residents.

To them, Philly Patch was a paradise. They remember it most fondly as a great place in which to have lived and to have grown up.

"The residents of Philly Patch were more like an extended family than anything else I can describe," said Shirley Borrelli, who, along with her late husband, Sam Borrelli Jr., raised two of their four children in the 14 years they lived there. "Everybody took care of everybody else's children.

"We knew our kids were safe," she added, "because everybody was watching. I don't care what other people thought it looked like, this was home to us and a darn good home it was."

The last of the 45 double homes was demolished more than 33 years ago, when the course of Chartiers Creek was changed via the multimillion-dollar Chartiers Creek Flood Control Project.

What's hard to imagine is that at one time, in the heart of the Great Depression, Philly Patch was hailed in a 1934 story in the now-defunct Canonsburg Daily Notes newspaper as a "model community." All 90 mine company-owned homes were remodeled inside and out and were equipped with "modern convenience," probably indoor plumbing and electricity.

Before Canonsburg Coal Co., successor to Chartiers Creek Mining Co., began remodeling Philly Patch, the settlement had slipped badly into

Above: Mary Livolsi (now Mary Boroch) and her baby doll pose in front of homes at Philadelphia Place. The area started out as New Philadelphia in the late 1890s, later being called "Philly Patch." By early 1973, every bit of the area was gone.

disrepair, a product of the hard times brought on by the Depression. Squatters, who had occupied a number of the homes there, were said only to have been "relocated," but the newspaper story doesn't say where.

All the homes in nearby Buffalo Patch, which clung to the side of a hill west of Weavertown Road overlooking, close-up, the Hazel Mine tipple and portal, were torn down. Usable lumber was salvaged and recycled to rehabilitate the best of what was left standing in Philly Patch.

What further set Philly Patch apart from other company towns in the region was that it was practically in downtown Canonsburg. After all, Hazel Mine, the mine that built the housing, was within a short walk down a long city block from downtown Canonsburg and the borough offices, the police department and fire station.

Imagine that, if you would, a coal patch town inside the borough proper, and an easy walk to what was then a vital and thriving downtown business district.

'When It Rains, It Pours'

Philadelphia Place flourished throughout the first half of the 20th century. Its ultimate fate was sealed, however, after Canonsburg's long-

Above: Among the neighborhood children in Philly Patch, dressed in Easter finery, were Delores Dobbin, Frankie, Tommy and Bobby Dobbin. Delores, who was know as "Dolly," grew up to marry Canonsburg singing legend Bobby Vinton. Others pictured include Mary and John Livolsi and Mary Jane Weippert.

remembered Flood of 1956, one of the many that the low-lying areas along Chartiers Creek suffered with regularity over the years. It took another 16 years or so after the '56 flood for Philly Patch to vanish completely.

An old saying (borrowed from the actual sales slogan for Morton Salt) that "when it rains, it pours - into the basements in Philly Patch," rang all too true. But by late 1972, and most certainly by early 1973, all of it was gone - every board, every brick, every outbuilding - as the result of an ambitious, long overdue, and highly successful flood control program. And costly, too.

The flood control project was the linchpin of the even broader, and far more costly Urban Renewal Project. More than $16 million in federal, state and local funds were used to straighten, dredge, widen and relocate the channel of Chartiers Creek, and to virtually remake Pike Street and Smith Street, from Ashland Avenue to near Greenside Avenue.

Philly Patch was in the way of the flood control project and redevelopment. It had to go, and it did.

Its passing is the classic example of addition by subtraction. On the 31 acres between the four sets of railroad tracks that bordered Adams Avenue and old Curry Hill Road (now Morganza Road), where the four rows of co-joined twin single-family homes stood for 70 years, now stands Canonsburg's "restaurant row."

The dredging, straightening and widening of Chartiers Creek meant both the end of Philly Patch and of flooding of near epic proportions. Best remembered as the worst floods were those of 1888, 1912 and 1956.

"I remember that 1956 flood very vividly," Borrelli said. "It rained and rained and the water from the creek started to come up. In the middle of the night, Sam and I put the kids on our shoulders and carried them out. We walked in water that came up to our waists.

"My father-in-law lived on Weavertown Road, maybe 200 yards away on the high ground," she continued. "They never got flooded over there, so that's where we took the kids when it rained and when the flooding came.

"That's also where we lived, too, while we waited for the water to go down and for us to get back into our house to clean out the mud and move back in again," she said.

Sol Toder, whose father, Sam, started a small auto parts salvage

Above: Behind John Livolsi is the house where Randa Patterson Cochran grew up in Philadelphia Place.

business on East College Street in 1926 and 10 years later moved it a block away to near the entrance to Philly Patch, remembers as a kid the flooding there.

"That damn place was always flooded," recalled Toder. "We had a night watchman who, when Chartiers Creek came over its banks, would just open the doors of the big building, our warehouse and the office, and let the water go through it."

Toder, who joined the business in 1954, right after college at Pitt and a stint in the U.S. Army, took over after his father had a heart attack. In

Above: Philadelphia Place, which was called New Philadelphia when it was built in the late 1800s, is surrounded by water from the flood of 1912.

1957-58, he moved the salvage yard - all the salvage cars, assorted parts including engines, transmissions, bumpers and fenders - out of the old Philly Patch location to make way for a modern, automated bowling alley, the Canon Bowl.

When the flood control project began a half-dozen years later, Canon Bowl - lock, stock and bowling lanes, everything - was purchased by Imperatore Enterprises. Rebuilt behind the former Imperatore Ford dealership, Canon Bowl became Jefferson Lanes.

"We had a little more than one acre of land down there," Toder explained referring to the salvage yard. "I know that people who can still remember the place think it was bigger than that, but that was it, just over an acre."

Toder bought a 5-plus acre piece of property along Route 19 in North Strabane Township, where he relocated the business, which is known today as Route 19 Auto Salvage. Toder sold the business to longtime employee Jim Dodd Jr. in 2001 and retired.

Practically all that remains of the Patch and of Toder's salvage yard are two mounted photographs on display on the wall inside Wendy's restaurant on

Cavasina Drive. One photo shows Toder's salvage yard. The photo is mislabeled as having been taken in 1950, when it is probably late 1955 or early '56, as a 1956 model Plymouth and a 1956 Chevrolet can be seen clearly in the photo.

On another wall is a photo of Philly Patch standing in the 1912 floodwater about four feet deep on the first floor of the houses, approximately where Wendy's now stands.

Terri Ritter, whose family was among the last to move out (Dec. 5, 1970, was moving day for them), said the flooding was just a part of living

Above: This aerial photograph shows the east end of Canonsburg at the intersection of College and Pike streets under water. It was this flood that proved to be the catalyst for the Chartiers Creek Flood Control Project. Philadelphia Place, only partially seen in the upper left corner, was a casualty of the project.

Left: View of Weavertown during Flood of 1912.

Above: Aerial view, facing east, shows redevelopment in progress in late 1972 n area surrounding what was once called Philadelphia Place, or "Philly Patch." Toward the top of the photo are a few houses remaining in Philly Patch.

there, to be dealt with when it happened, to be tolerated if only barely.

"We knew it was going to flood whenever big rains started," she said. "For us, it was a way of life. If we were the only ones who got flooded, we would have moved out. But it happened to all of us, and we all pulled together to get through it.

"It's really hard for people to understand what living there was like," she said. "To us, Philly Patch was the best neighborhood in Canonsburg with the best people. That's how

we felt. You can't find people like that now, I'm sure."

Jenice Markovich Vesely, Terri Ritter's daughter, fondly recalls her friends in Philly Patch. One of her friends was Dolores Dobbins, who years later married singer Bobby Vinton.

"As a matter of fact," said the resident of McMurray and now a secretary in the Peters Township School District, "my first boyfriend was her brother, Robby Dobbins. He was cute."

Mary Livolsi Boroch, Randa Patterson Cochran and Rose Marie Gordon grew up playing together in Philly Patch. Now they work together in the offices of Washington County Children and Youth and often talk about their days there. The Livolsis and Pattersons were neighbors; Rose Marie's

Above: Aerial view of the Chartiers Creek Flood Control Project, which eliminated flooding in low-lying areas of Canonsburg, and resulted in the razing of the former Philly Patch.

Left: View of East Canonsburg taken from Buffalo Hill to the left of the present Weavertown Road during the mid-1930s. Todar's salvage yard can be seen in the center left of the photo; Philadelphia Place is at center right.

grandparents, Tom and Lydia Welsh, lived there also. She visited them often, sometimes just to play with Mary and Randa.

"If we were poor, we didn't know about it," Boroch said. "Nobody was better off than anybody else, black or white. We were all friends and neighbors."

"We were really, really close as kids," Cochran said. "We were best friends growing up and we're still friends. We owe that to where we grew up and the people who raised us."

Bruce Borrelli, Shirley's son, was only 7 when his family moved out of Philly Patch, but they didn't go far, just a block away.

"Even though we moved, Philly Patch was still my favorite place to go until I was 15 and they started to tear the place down," he said. "We fished in Chartiers Creek every day and we played ball on Curry Field. We'd play 'war' and 'hide and seek' in everybody's yards. And we all went to Charnick's store, just across the Weavertown Bridge. We collected pop bottles throughout the Patch and we'd use the money to buy penny candy from Mr. Charnick.

"If you lived in Philly Patch, you had a great childhood," said Borelli, 47, who owns a car lot at the intersection of Interstate 79 and Route 519, Houston-Hill Church Road, near Canonsburg Hospital. "Ask any of us who lived there. They'll all tell you the same."

And they did. Too bad it's all gone now. Good thing the memories live on.

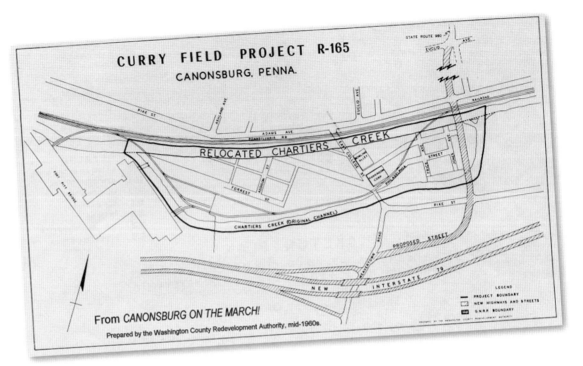

Above: The Curry Field Urban Renewal Project effectively solved the flooding problem. The primary objectives were to create an industrial park, relocate and widen Chartiers Creek, and construct a ramp to Interstate 79. Phase 1, downstream from Canonsburg, was the first part completed in July 1970. Work on the creek from the Bridge Works to Houston began in April 1970, and the third phase, Bridge Works to Brush Run, had a completion date of 1973. The map, from "Canonsburg on the March!" promotional brochure, shows the old and new creek beds. A different street plan, with the bridge near the mouth of Euclid Avenue, was eventually used.

Right: John Thomas outside his home at Philadelphia Place, or "Philly Patch," during the August 6, 1956, flood. Photograph by Joseph A. Solobay.

Poor Farm

Published December 12, 2004
The County Home in Waynesburg was a respectable place where the indigent could reside with dignity.

By Denise Bachman

Andy the Shoemaker was a pleasant soul who operated a coffee/shoe repair shop in the "dungeons" on what was commonly known as the poor farm in Greene County.

Aside from his customers, he also counted among his faithful companions the intoxicated residents, who were regularly tossed in the dungeons until they sobered up following a night of merrymaking with local miners in Bobtown.

One sultry, summer day, Andy the Shoemaker was asked to retrieve some vegetables from the backyard garden. When he didn't return, a "search crew" was dispersed, only to find that the softened earth - courtesy of a particularly wet summer - had swallowed much of Andy's body and was holding him captive.

You see, Andy the Shoemaker had a wooden leg, and he quickly fell victim to Mother Nature's unintentional trap.

Left: The County Home in Waynesburg, commonly known as the poor farm, as it appears today. The poor farm, the County Home in Waynesburg was a respectable place where the indigent could reside with dignity. It was established in 1861, with 57 adults working there in return for hot meals and a warm bed. It closed in 1964, and reopened seven years later as the Greene County Historical Museum.

This is just one of several nuggets that have been told to Brenda Giles, administrator of the Greene County Historical Museum, which is housed in the former poor farm on Rolling Meadows Road in Franklin Township.

Despite its compelling 103-year history as a county home, the farmhouse and 52-room addition contain only remnants from those bygone days.

A few invoices, photographs and documents are displayed in the museum's Main Street exhibit in a corridor where residents of the poor farm once slept, but today the museum serves primarily as a repository for family heirlooms and other county treasures, 90 percent of which have been donated.

"Everybody here wanted it to be a fancy mansion, and it isn't," said Giles, pointing to the elaborate border paper in the main parlor. "The poor farm is the richest part of its history."

The property consists of 147 acres that were patented in the 1760s as Lions Bush. In 1850, Robinson and Catherine Downey, who owned the Downey House Hotel building on Washington Street in downtown Waynesburg, purchased the farmhouse and the land surrounding it, then sold it for $5,000 to the county, which had been directed by law in 1859 to erect and support a house of employment for the indigent.

The "inmates," as they were called in early documentation because, Giles surmises, they were considered wards of the state, were to be managed by a steward and matron appointed by three directors of the poor, each of whom was paid $200 a year.

Hence, the poor farm, or the County Home as it was officially called, was established in 1861, with 57 adults working there in return for hot meals and a warm bed. They sewed, they tended the fields and they raised livestock.

"They did all that they were capable of doing," said Giles, noting that some residents were mentally retarded.

By 1880, there were 91 residents living in only

Above: Several male residents of the County Home in Waynesburg in the 1950s.

16 small rooms. Dr. A.J. Ourt, secretary for the State Committee of Lunacy, called the poor farm a "den of bugs and vermin ... the worst building in the state." His comments were published by the Atlantic Monthly in a story headlined "The Indoor Pauper: A Study."

In response, the Waynesburg Republican launched a campaign for reform, and in 1882, a

Above: Several female residents of the County Home, or poor farm, in Waynesburg in the 1950s.

grand jury mandated an addition to accommodate 100 people and modernization of the heating and ventilation systems in the bathrooms.

By 1888, $7,299 worth of additions - including a kitchen and laundry facilities, plus a large auditorium for church services - were completed, and the poor farm received a favorable report in July

Above: Oliver Hewitt holds a rifle and a dead groundhog.

1889 following an inspection by the State Board of Charities.

The Good Life

Based on photographs, some first-hand recollections and stories passed from generation to generation, life on the poor farm actually was good.

"It was back when people took care of each other," Giles said. "When you look at the photos, you don't feel bad for those people. They were fed and cared for very well."

In fact, by the early 1900s, appropriations to the County Home and the Children's Home - built for orphans in 1884 on an 80-acre farm in Morgan Township - usually were the largest expenditures in the county's budget, according to G. Wayne Smith in "History of Greene County Pennsylvania." In 1906, for example, the two homes received $11,000 from the county; by 1922, that figure more than doubled to $22,700.

"There are no bad memories in the 1930s and 1940s," Giles said. "It was like having an extended family."

Administrator Oliver Hewitt and his wife, Mary, who shared the main farmhouse with staff, can take credit for that. Barbershop quartets and the Waynesburg Citizens Band regularly performed for the residents, and the food was so good that the county commissioners, who in 1938 began to manage the home when the directors of the poor were eliminated, often visited to partake of a meal.

In addition, a barber and teacher regularly visited the poor farm. According to one of the

Above: Oliver Hewitt was longtime administrator of the poor farm, officially called the County Home, in the 1930s and '40s.

ledgers, in 1921, Isaac Stahl was paid $168 to cut hair, and Margaret Scott earned $375 teaching school there.

Men and women lived in separate quarters, as did the mentally retarded.

Like most people, 82-year-old Frances Clister of Wind Ridge fondly recalls her days working as a cook for the Hewitts.

"The whole bunch was really nice. I really

liked the people I worked for," she said. "I remember getting a picture of Mr. Hewitt on a scooter."

Mrs. Clister started to work at the poor farm in the late 1930s at the age of 16, riding her bike from Stringtown, near Carmichaels. She had little interaction with the residents because she primarily worked in the main house.

"I'd get there in the mornings, and my scarf would be covered with ice," she said. "I know one thing. When I couldn't go by bike, I went on a bus, then I hitchhiked back.

"I worked there a long time. I remember we had a great big cook stove. I wish I could remember names."

Bill Hewitt of Wind Ridge, a member of the board of directors at the Greene County Historical Society, is a distant relative of Oliver Hewitt: Oliver Hewitt's father and Bill Hewitt's great-grandfather were brothers.

More importantly, though, Bill Hewitt's grandmother, Gail McCartney, was the head cook for 12 years in the 1950s and '60s and shared a bedroom there. Bill Hewitt would frequently visit his grandmother, and he would hang out with Oliver Hewitt's grandson.

"I have a lot of memories and I remember how nice everybody was, even the people who were living there as guests of the poor farm," said Hewitt, now 68. "That's a part of my life, and I'm always happy to tell people about it.

"I'd just go down, visit my grandmother and visit everybody else. I stayed there a night or two, and they more or less adopted me."

Above: Several female residents of the County Home, or poor farm, in Waynesburg in the 1950s.

Right: Several male residents of the County Home in Waynesburg in the 1950s.

Right: Gail McCartney, left, head cook at the poor farm in the 1950s and '60s, with fellow cooks. Her grandson, Bill Hewitt, remembers visiting her at the County Home and now resides in Wind Ridge.

Below: Bill Hewitt of Wind Ridge, a member of the board of directors at the Greene County HIstorical Society, is a distant relative of Oliver Hewitt (Oliver Hewitt's father and Bill great-grandfather were brothers), who was administrator of the poor farm in the 1930s and 1940s.

Hungry For Respect

Even though the County Home, which later was called the Greene County Home for the Aged, was known as the poor farm, Hewitt said it wasn't meant to be "derogatory" in any way; it was just a place for people with little education and no family to call home.

"They put on some good meals down there - the sheriff, commissioners, there were a whole bunch who would come. It was a nice place," he said. "I always felt welcome, and as a kid, it's really part of my background."

Hewitt said his grandmother baked her own bread and made homemade butter. She, along with the staff, also canned their own vegetables.

The kitchen for the inmates was what is now the museum store, and the lengthy dining hall now contains myriad county-related displays. The museum office once was Oliver Hewitt's office, and the music room was the sitting room.

"I remember the poor farm people being taken care of. They were treated with respect. There was no animosity," Hewitt said. "The people there worked. If they were able, they helped outside. They did a lot of farming, milked cows and provided food. The ladies worked in the back kitchen. The general feeling was that these people had a good home and were very happy to be there.

"Taxpayers weren't burdened with it, and Mr. and Mrs. Hewitt were probably two of the kindest people I knew. They'd get out there and work with them. They treated everybody as equals. I think if any of these people were alive today, they'd tell you they were happy to have a place to stay."

Giles was told one resident spent her life on the poor farm after she was injured in a car accident. Other residents, though, were occasionally released to relatives, who were required to sign a document that stated they would take full responsibilty for his care so he would not "become again a charge upon the poor district."

Until the end of World War II, the poor farm population was basically a younger bunch, as women whose husbands went to war moved in. Also, there were times when men would leave the farm to look for jobs and never return.

Although Giles can't confirm that children lived at the poor farm, and one document states that women were permitted to stay in the home for only six months after giving birth, one of the ledgers proves otherwise.

In 1921, children - six boys and three girls - lived in the home for the first time, and during that year, 10 boys and six girls were admitted, and seven boys and four girls were dismissed.

Then there is the tragic tale of a baby's death at the hands of one of the residents. After dinner one evening, the staff and residents discovered a strange smell coming from the oven. One of the mentally retarded residents said she was cooking a turkey. But when the oven was opened, no turkey was found. It was a baby.

By the 1950s, most of the poor farm residents were elderly, and those who needed extended care had been moved to Curry Memorial Home, which opened across the road in December 1931. It operated for nearly 60 years until construction was completed on Rolling Meadows Nursing Home, where some residents were later transferred.

"In the 1950s, 20-some people lived at the poor farm," Giles said. "It was more of a retirement facility."

The poor farm finally closed in 1964, and seven years later, it reopened as the Greene County Historical Museum.

"I think it's one of the great treasures we have in Greene County," Hewitt said. "It might have been called a poor farm, but it was rich in a lot of other things."

Above: The Greene County Historical Society Museum, built in the 1850s, was a typical Greene County farmhouse made of locally fired brick. In the late 1800s, several wings were added and it became the poor farm to house the county's indigents. They planted crops and raised farm animals that fed them. The county leased the building to the Historical Society in 1969 and it opened as a museum in 1971.

Right: Andy the Shoemaker, who had a wooden leg, operated a coffee/shoe repair shop in the largest room in the dungeons - first door on the left - at the poor farm. The other rooms were used to house drunken residents until they sobered.

Voices with a Smile

Published March 19, 2006
Before technological advances, anybody who made a phone call
was guaranteed to speak with a live person.

By Denise Bachman

Peruse her high school yearbook, and you'll find that Lizz Sobansky's career ambition was to be a telephone operator.

So, when she was hired by Bell Telephone Co. in 1950 to work in its Washington central office, she was very happy, to say the least.

"I always wanted to be a telephone operator. I felt very honored when I got hired," said Sobansky, who resides in Washington.

The reason, she said, was simple: She liked to talk and help people.

"I've always been glad I worked for the phone company," said Sobansky, who logged a total of 23 years with Bell and AT&T, interrupting her career for a few years to raise her children. "At times, I'd like to go back. I would do it all over again."

Before technological advances brought us answering machines and automated telephone systems, anybody who made a telephone call was guaranteed to speak with a live person. In fact, telephone operators became known as voices with a smile, whose commitment to friendly customer service was paramount.

Left: Telephone calls in 1941 were handled by a bank of operators squeezed into a tight row at the Washington central office at Main and Beau streets.

To that end, supervisors constantly walked behind the operators to make sure they were doing their job.

"That didn't bother us," said Jessie Wood of Washington, who worked for the phone company for 35 years. "Sometimes, the supervisors would pull up a chair and plug into the board, just to see what we were doing."

There were three basic rules: Don't chew gum, don't talk to your co-workers and, above all, be courteous.

"We gave polite service. We were very professional," Wood said. "We had one common goal: to serve the customer. It was service, service, service."

Making the connection

According to The Reporter, Dana Hubbard and Professor Wright made the first long-distance connection in Washington on May 13, 1877, when, on their second attempt in two days, they were able to carry on a conversation between Washington and Wheeling, W.Va. The conversation took place just 14 months after the first complete sentence was transmitted over the telephone by inventor Alexander Graham Bell.

The first telephone exchange office in Washington was established by the Central District and Printing Telegraph Co. on Oct. 21, 1884, in the W.C. Briceland building at 66 W. Wheeling St. The switchboard was a two-position magneto type, meaning callers had to lift their telephone receivers and crank the handle to ring into the operator, who, at the time, was Jennie Rodgers. Her office hours were 7:30 a.m. to noon; 1 to 5 p.m.; and 6 to 8 p.m.

According to The Reporter, credit for the birth of the Washington exchange belongs to H.U. Seaman, a local jeweler who, with some difficulty, managed to obtain the required 50 subscribers who were willing to pay $60 per year for telephone service. Telephone No. 1 was in the house of A.J. Montgomery, which is now 700 Allison Ave. Other subscribers and their telephone numbers included Washington Seminary, 5; Julius LeMoyne, 10; Reporter office, 16; Trinity Hall, 17;

Auld House, 30; Observer office, 31, and Gantz Mill, 38.

Two telephone conversations, believed to be the first made at the Washington exchange, were preserved by Bell Telephone Co. The first occurred between Seaman and Robert Wolfe of the Wheeling Telephone Co.

"Homer Seaman?"

"Hello. What do you want?"

"I want you to send me that silver dish I was looking at this morning."

"I'll do it. Want any engraving on it?"

"Not today. Some other day. Good day."

"Good day."

The other conversation between LeMoyne and J.A. Howden was recorded as follows:

"Hello, LeMoyne."

"Hello. Is that you Howden?"

Above: First underground telephone line conduit being built in Washington in 1906. View looking up Beau Street toward Main Street from Schaeffer Alley.

Right: The telephone company operated its Washington central office from 49 Strawberry Alley for 10 years before moving to the third floor of the Washington Trust Building in 1907. It later relocated to 41 East Beau Street.

"Yes. A lot of your sheep have escaped from the pasture field and are now in danger."

"Much obliged. I'll come down and take care of them."

In 1897, the Washington central office moved to 49 Strawberry Ave., and 10 years later, it moved to the third floor of the Washington Trust Building. Also in 1907, the switchboard changed from a magneto type to a common battery system in which a light would be activated whenever someone wanted to place a call.

In 1918, the Washington office became part of Bell Telephone Co., and eventually it relocated to 41 E. Beau St. By 1952, the Washington office was serving 28,000 customers in the area and handling a daily average of 95,000 local calls and 2,800 toll calls.

On Dec. 2, 1956, dial service began in Washington.

"That was a major change because all the instruments had to be changed and you no longer would hear the melodious voice saying, 'Number, please,'" John Duskey of Washington said.

Duskey began his career with Bell of Pennsylvania on Feb. 9, 1953, as an installer and was the director of external affairs when he retired Nov. 1, 1995 – just three months shy of his 43-year anniversary – with plenty of fond memories.

Bell answers call

"We were the telephone company. Nobody else was allowed by law to manufacture or connect phones," Duskey said. "Bell was obligated to provide service to everybody." In addition, repairs were free and telephones were replaced for free.

Duskey said he remembers the 5-cent phone calls and coin-operated phones, but "the most significant number in my mind is when we went to dial service. It cost $2.64 a month for a four-party line."

Before the dial service, coin-operated phones were on every corner.

"We liked it that way," said Albena "Beanie" Angott of Washington, who worked 13 years full time and two years part time for the phone company. She also put the last telephone-operator assisted call through from Claysville in November 1974.

In their heyday, each telephone operator at the Washington central office would field about 200 calls an hour, depending, of course, on the time of day. There were five different switchboards – incoming, outgoing, information, long distance and local – and each was covered 24 hours a day, with as many as 20 operators handling just the local calls during the busy 8-to-5 shift. When Sobansky was hired in

Left: Two switchboard operators were able to handle the volume of calls in Burgettstown in 1914.

1950, Bell employed 200 operators at its Washington central office.

Operators were constantly monitored to ensure they were expediting every call. The number of signals it took them to answer was recorded and reviewed every half-hour.

Each operator was trained for a specific job, and when business slowed, they received new job training. For example, Kay Popeck of Washington started her 39-year career with the phone company as a long-distance operator. She spent three weeks in training, learning rates, routing numbers and documentation. (Every long-distance call had to be documented on paper, complete with the operator's employee number.)

After working long distance for a while, Popeck learned how to handle local calls. "In an emergency, they would pull you from one station to another," she said.

That's what happened to Sobansky and Wood while they were working incoming calls one New Year's Eve.

"There were no calls coming in. They told us to go to another switchboard," Sobansky said. "We ran. We would rather be busy."

No time to snoop

Telephone operators also were required to sign a confidentiality agreement known as "secrecy of communication" when they were hired. Every six months, the agreement was reviewed and had to be signed again.

But, according to Frances Knestrick, eavesdropping on callers' conversations was never a problem.

"We were so busy, we had no time to listen in," said Knestrick, a 22-year veteran who eventually became a supervisor.

The only exception, she said, was when an operator was asked to interrupt a telephone conversation for an emergency. An operator, along with a supervisor, would monitor the call to prove it was an emergency.

This, said Lil Varner of Washington, reduced the number of prank calls they received.

One longtime supervisor, Clara M. Shaffer, was a strict disciplinarian, but she started a 10-year club for telephone operators in 1942 and encouraged them to do volunteer work in the community.

To this day, members of the club remain a close bunch – they consider themselves more like family – and the club has more than 100 members. It also has expanded its membership to all telephone operators, regardless of years of service.

"Miss Shaffer was a task master," Jessie Wood said. "I was half afraid of her and half in admiration of her. I always regarded her with profound respect. She was a very, very great lady. When she walked into the room, she sucked the oxygen out."

Wood said Shaffer would be pleased that 64 years later, the club is still going strong. The matriarch of the club is 89-year-old Audra Fullerton of Washington, who retired as a manager after 39 years of service. She earned $7 a week during the Depression, and she didn't have a phone in her home when she started to work for the phone company.

"For us to remain as we have for this many years is a tribute to the phone company," said Wood, noting that she and her colleagues always had the utmost respect for their supervisors and the company.

If, for example, there was a shortage of operators, no matter what time you were called, Wood said an operator reported for duty.

Left: Operators handle calls at the Washington Central office in 1941.

"You'd cut your tongue out before you'd say you don't want to work," Wood said. "We felt privileged to work there."

Local exchanges

Each central office was equipped with an alpha/numeric designation when they were established. The letters of the exchange name corresponded to the letters on the rotary dial of the telephone. The first two letters of the exchange name, plus the exchange number were known as the Named Number Exchange. For example, the NNX for Washington was 222 and 225, and was derived by combining the first two letters, plus the number of its exchange names: Baldwin 2 and Baldwin 5. Since B is 2 on the telephone dial and A is 2, Baldwin 2 became 222 and Baldwin 5 became 225. John Duskey of Washington, a longtime employee of Bell of Pennsylvania, said naming the exchange provided a personal identity with each community and made it easier to recognize and retain numbers for dialing.

Other area NNXs were:
- Avella – Luther 7 (587)
- Burgettstown – Whitney 7 (947)
- Canonsburg – Sherwood 5 (745)
- Claysville – Normandy 3 (663)
- McDonald – Wasbash 6 (926)
- McMurray – Wilson 1 (941)
- Oakdale – Owens 3 (693)
- West Alexander – Huxley 4 (484)

Above: From left, Charles Hamilton of the Washington Street Department, Bell Plant Wire Chief Robert D. Bruce, Administrative Assistant to Washington City Council Neil Blanton and Washington Sub-District Manager Stanley B. Ross watch as Washington Mayor T.S. Fitch places the first telephone call over the new Baldwin dial system.

Right: Telephone operators participated in various charitable projects. Displaying slipper socks they made for the needy at Christmas in 1959 are, seated, Albena "Beanie" Angott, left, and Rose Kelly; standing, from left, Grace DeMay, Mary Reinbold, Florence Bradley and Annabelle Sams.

The First Hundred Years of
Pennsylvania's Finest

Published May 1, 2005
Commonwealth boasts the first state police organization in the country

By Kathie O. Warco

Labor strife at the turn of the 20th century prompted the creation of what would become the first state police unit in the United States.

The men and women who wear the patch of Pennsylvania State Police Trooper on their gray uniforms marked the agency's 100th year in 2005.

Pennsylvania Gov. Samuel W. Pennypacker signed a law creating the state police on May 2, 1905, on the heels of the Great Anthracite Strike three years earlier.

In the years before the coal strike, industrialists and their employees often were at odds. The coal and steel operators persuaded the state Legislature to authorize the creation of the Coal and Iron Police. For $1 each, the state sold the mine and steel mill owners commission to give police power to whomever the operators selected. While armies of guards were raised through the commissions to protect private property, they were more likely to enforce the will of owners.

Left: This photo of Pennsylvania State Police, Troop D mounted, Punxsutawney, is part of the memorabilia collection of Jay Bedillion, a police communications operator for the last 12 years with state police at Troop B headquarters in Washington.

According to the state police Web site, "common gunmen, hoodlums and adventurers were hired to fill these commissions and they served their own interests by causing violence and terror."

After the strike, it was determined that peace should be kept by regularly appointed officers employed by the public. The original stations were in Greensburg (Troop A), Wilkes-Barre, later in Wyoming (Troop B), Reading (Troop C) and Punxsutawney (Troop D), with orders to patrol the state's entire 45,000 square miles.

While there were concerns from labor that the state police would be used as a private army, the original complement of officers was limited to 228 men. Today, the force exceeds 4,600 sworn members and 1,600 civilian personnel.

In spite of the concerns, the organizational structure and operation of the department were much like the military. Men recently out of the police academy were enlisted at the rank of private. Other ranks included corporal, sergeant, lieutenant, captain and major. During the 100-year history of the state police, the head of the agency was known either as superintendent or commissioner. Today, the commissioner holds the rank of colonel.

Almost 50 years after the state police was founded, when he graduated from the state police academy, Keith McCulley found that it still ran very much like a military operation. Many of the cadets had a military background.

"But it was still a rough six months," McCulley, of Washington, said of the training. "Some didn't make it through."

After graduation in November 1951, the 22-year-old private second class was assigned to Troop B headquarters, which was relocated to Washington in 1938. The city directory shows that for a time, the barracks was located at 530 S. Main St., Washington, near West Prospect Avenue, before eventually moving to its current site on Murtland Avenue in 1948.

To enlist, applicants had to be single. They were not permitted to marry until they had been enlisted for two years and only after receiving permission from their commanding officer. Their brides also were subject to a background check to make sure they were fit.

George Barron of Kane, McKean County, and a member of McCulley's class at the academy, remembers getting permission to marry his wife, Jean. Barron, a native of Pittsburgh's South Side and a regular visitor to Washington County, provides annual training for California University of Pennsylvania police officers.

"My wife always laughs because I had to submit a letter to the troop commander," said Barron, who also was 22 when he joined the academy. "And since she is not Catholic, I had to get dispensation from the Catholic Church to enter a mixed marriage. But she said I never did ask her dad for permission to marry her."

Barron said that before marrying, enlisted officers had to

Above: Traffic accidents are part of routine work for state police.

Right: Members of Pennsylvania State Police Troop C in 1936.

promise their marriage would not interfere with their duties.

"We stayed at the barracks, where there were two bunks in each bedroom and a mess hall with three cooks who prepared three meals a day," McCulley said, adding that the former bedrooms are now used as offices at the Washington station. "If you were married, you still had to sleep in the barracks unless it was your day off.

"We worked six days a week. Sometimes the shift would be split and we'd work 8 a.m. to noon and 4 p.m. to midnight," he added. "One guy would be in the patrol car except on midnight."

Living together had its benefits. "We were all pretty close," McCulley said. "We were more like a family."

McCulley said they were expected to be at the

Above: Mounted state police officers on patrol. Part of the memorabilia collection of Jay Bedillion, a police communications operator for the last 12 years with state police at Troop B headquarters in Washington.

MEMBERS-TROOP "C" 1936 PENNA. STATE POLICE

CAPT. SAMUEL W. GEARHART   LIEUT. EDWIN C. GRIFFITH

1st Sgt. Edward C. Sickel

barracks for roll call even on their day off. It wasn't until the early to mid-1960s that the state police went to a five-day work week under the direction of Commissioner Col. E. Wilson Purdy.

"They said that wouldn't work," he added. "But it did."

The starting salary for privates was $150 a month, less deductions for income tax. After three years of service, they were promoted to private first class. The private classification was replaced by "trooper" in 1956. Married personnel, on the job for at least four years, could request permission to be given a subsistence and quarters allowance of $2 day. Once they were granted subsistence, they were no longer eligible for meals provided by the state at the barracks.

It wasn't until 1963 that the state police changed regulations to allow married men to apply for admission. That also was the same year the requirement for re-enlistment every two years was discontinued.

McCulley spent 17 of his 36-year career in Troop B, including as its commander from 1977-87, when he retired. Barron spent most of his career in the northern and central part of the state before retiring as a sergeant in 1978.

When McCulley came to Washington in November 1951 from Clearfield, trolleys were cling-clanging along the streets of the city. Route 19, for the most part, was still a two-lane road, and there were no interstates. Substations were located in Imperial, Belle Vernon, Uniontown and Waynesburg.

Privates were never assigned close to their hometown. "I think they did that so we wouldn't know anyone," McCulley said.

McCulley said crimes back then ranged from burglaries to murders to thefts. The troop also was called to assist at incidents at Western Penitentiary, including a few riots and a hostage situation.

When McCulley joined, the officers were dispatched to calls by radio. Such was not the case in the early days. In the 1920s, police worked with owners of telephones in patrol zones. The owners of the phones were given flags or steel disks to display when a call was received, and the patrol officer would call the station for assignments.

While horses are now used by state police only for special activities, including crowd control, cadets continue to learn equestrian basics at the training academy. Horses were the means of transportation for the state police in the early days. The animals were well-trained: They were taught to "play dead," which entailed lying down noiselessly and jumping back up when signalled.

"Some of the guys just couldn't take to the horses," McCulley said.

McCulley, who was used to horses while growing up, participated in the annual rodeo held each summer at Hershey. "It was quite an event," McCulley said. "I'd go and ride in it every summer."

Over the years, state police had several different names. It was formed as the state police in 1905, became the Pennsylvania State Highway

Right Top, Middle, and Bottom: Privates used motorcycles and patrol cars as early modes of transportation.

The First Hundred Years of Pennsylvania's Finest

Patrol in 1923, the Pennsylvania Motor Patrol in 1937 and back to state police in 1943.

Both Barron and McCulley enjoyed their careers. "It was a good career," said McCulley. "I wouldn't have changed anything."

Barron joined the state police after a stint in the U.S. Coast Guard. He was inspired by a neighbor, who was a member of the state police motorcycle unit.

"He was my idol, but I joined because I wanted to do something to make Pennsylvania a better and safer place, as corny as that may sound," Barron said.

Above: Students attend class at the state police academy in 1961.

Left: Exterior of the state police academy building in 1961.

Baseball Die-Hards

Published July 31, 2005

By Doug Street

Baseball, in its purest form, hasn't changed much over the years.

The bases are still 90 feet apart; the pitcher's mound, 60 feet, 6 inches from home plate. Three strikes, three outs and nine innings all are staples of the game that have stood the test of time.

Aesthetically, though, baseball has changed quite a bit. The pristine fields and multimillion-dollar complexes that dot the local landscape are a far cry from years past.

Organized teams are abundant for the younger players, but from there, players suddenly leave the game as they grow older.

There was a time when many local players carried their love of playing the game well into their 30s and 40s. Although a few adult baseball leagues still exist today, back in the 1930s through '50s, adult baseball leagues were a dominant source of recreation.

Sandlots were alive, not with the sounds of children learning the sport, but of men still stoking the fires of their passion to play the game they loved.

Left: Ron Necciai (standing, third from left) is shown in 1949 with the Monongahela American Legion team, which went on to win the state championship a year later. Necciai, who played in the minor leagues for the Pittsburgh Pirates, and sand lot ball, lives in Monongahela.

In the Beginning

After the Great Depression, the economy began to pick up and more people were back at work. For children growing up then, baseball - or some form of it, more likely stickball - was a cheap and easy form of exercise and entertainment.

As the 1930s wore on, there were those who made their way into the workplace but still had a desire to keep playing. It was then that leagues such as the Washington Community, Washington County and Suburban baseball leagues began to form.

"Most everybody worked eight hours or more during the days, and on nights or weekends, we went out after work and played the game of baseball," said Billy Reese, a standout player who graduated from Washington High School in 1943 and played on the sandlots throughout the '40s. "We really enjoyed it."

Once the leagues began forming, it didn't take long for the popularity to grow tremendously.

Nowadays, every youth league has registration; parents pay the required fee and there is a spot on the team. That wasn't always the case.

"In the spring, you had to earn your way onto a team or you wouldn't play," said Robert Ruchell, a Washington resident who began playing in the adult leagues as a 17-year-old in 1944, before going off to serve in World War II. After returning home, he played another 10 years before finding his way to the slow-pitch softball leagues.

"Usually in the spring, the numbers would be pretty high and it was tough to get on a team because they could only have a certain number of players," Ruchell said.

The Players

"We had some great ballplayers," said Harry "Mousey" McKee, a longtime sandlot player who as the years passed kept the memory of the leagues alive with the Old-Timer's Baseball Association, a group of former players who met once a year to re-live the glory days.

"We had several that either went away and played in the minor leagues or came back after they played professionally and played in the leagues."

Perhaps the best-known name from the area is Stan Musial, the Donora native who went on to a Hall of Fame career with the St. Louis Cardinals.

Though Musial bypassed the local leagues for the big time, there were others who did both. One who made it to the majors was Edward "Babe" Butka, a Canonsburg native who played with the Washington Senators.

Butka was born in Canonsburg in 1916 and was a late-season callup in 1943. He played sparingly that season for the Senators and the next as well. In 18 major-league games, Butka, a 6-foot-3, 193-pound first baseman, hit .220 (11-for-50) with no home runs and one run batted in.

Butka also played in the minors for Williamsport in 1945 before settling back to Washington County. He died in April 2005 at age 89.

Also on that list from Donora is Ron Necciai, who still has a place in Organized Baseball history as the only man to strike out 27 batters in a nine-inning game, when he was pitching for Bristol in the Appalachian League in 1952. Necciai, who pitched for the Pirates later that season, makes his home in Monongahela.

The Teams

It took some time for the leagues to start gaining a foothold in the region. Money was tight and the players did what they had to do to get by.

"If you had a uniform, you were lucky," McKee recalled of the early days.

The fields also took some time to take shape. Reese recalled the field in Muse with an inch of dust over the infield, and when the ball hit it, the dust would not only kick up but the ball would skim across it, making it hard to field.

"They could be rough," McKee said. "If they were kept up they were OK, but some of them had pebbles which could make it rough to field the ball cleanly."

Above: Old Timers baseball, 1948; mascots George Glenn and Anthony DiPaolo. Front row, Jerome Brody, James Tucker, Dutch Kiefer, Scotty McVicker, Jinx Lazzari, Caddy Fisher, Ralph Cowan. Back row, Al Tosi, coach Gummy Pezzoni, unidentified, Wally Stearns, Amie Byers, John Balog, Joe Barboa, unidentified, Steve Nagy, Scissors McIlvain, Teddy "Bear" Zanardelli, stooped over also Dumpy Hamilton; also George Ostrander and Harry Sickels, "coach."

Above: A sandlot baseball team from the Mon Valley, circa 1905.

None of the fields had lights in those days, either.

"Sometimes the games would run late and we would put candles all around the fence so we could keep playing," McKee said.

As time went by, local businesses pitched in and sponsored most of the teams. Jessop Steel, Grief Dairy, Washington Steel, Alpine Club, Scott Motors and Washington Mould were some of the companies that sponsored teams. Leagues and teams in Canonsburg, Muse, Cecil and across Greene County sprang up as well. As such, most teams soon had uniforms, although they were made of wool, and during the hot summer months the wool mixed with sweat made the uniforms, as nice as they were,

quite unbearable.

"Man, they were hot," McKee said. "I was catching one game, it was 105 degrees and I nearly passed out."

The uniforms got better, and so did the fields. The Washington Community League played at Washington High School's field while the County League played at Washington Park. Those fields were better maintained, but as the seasons wore on even the nice fields took a beating.

"They did scrape them once in a while," Reese said. "Everyone was in the same batter's box and most everybody dug in at the plate. After a while the holes got pretty deep and you either had to stand in the hole or stand cockeyed in the box."

Softballs Make Hard Times

As the 1950s wore on, the number of players in the leagues began to dwindle. Other diversions such as television and going out to the movies began to entertain people more than a night playing baseball.

During the '50s, slow-pitch softball leagues began to form. The game was easier to play; it could be played by both men and women; and players could stay at a higher skill level well into their 40s, 50s, even 60s.

"Definitely, what hurt the sandlots was the slow-pitch softball. It came along and took over," Ruchell said. "There were still players around who were good enough to play baseball, but they went to softball instead."

There are some adult baseball leagues that still exist today, including the Washington Adult Baseball over-30 league. Others around the area include the Daily News League in the Mon Valley, the Federation League around Pittsburgh and the Fayette County League.

But the players of old don't think the leagues that were so prominent at one time will stage a comeback.

"I doubt it very much," Ruchell said. "The kids have so many other things to do now. They drive automobiles and a lot have jobs. Back then, we were pretty confined to where we lived.

"Besides, now these kids play Little League, the Pony League, then Colt League and high school, they are kind of tired of playing baseball. And as 18-year-olds, most of them are finished."

Movie Memories

Published May 16, 2004
Tri-State Drive-In stirs fond recollections.

By Brad Hundt

Part of the marquee stands in what is now the front yard of a private residence, but the "E" in "State" has long-since fallen away, and some of its bricks are missing. There's still an aluminum sign advertising it on a pole next to Route 18, and it taps rhythmically against a nearby utility pole when the breeze picks up.

The old screen is still standing, its white paint slowly peeling away. An 18-wheeler picking up frozen food from next-door Panhandle Food Sales idled underneath it during a recent afternoon. The seven-acre site that once could accommodate 500 cars on a busy Saturday night now has a "No Trespassing" sign up and is home only to a stray rabbit or two.

A few poles that once held speakers can be seen. They lean toward the ground like weather-beaten tombstones. The buildings that once held the concession stand, restrooms and projection booth all have vines growing on them and padlocks on the doors.

The Tri-State Drive-In was one of five drive-in theaters in Washington County. The others were the Mt. Lebanon Twin in McMurray; the Route 19 Drive-In outside Washington, now the site of the Cameron Wellness Center; the Hilltop Drive-In in Monongahela; and the Sunset Drive-In in Claysville. In Greene County, the Waynesburg Drive-In sat on the west side of town. The Skyview Drive-In is still open in Carmichaels.

It's forlorn and decrepit now, but when the Tri-State opened on July 1, 1955, with the Debbie Reynolds musical "Hit the Deck," it was touted as "the Cadillac of Drive-Ins."

An ad in that day's Washington Reporter promised it would be "the most modern drive-in in the tri-state area."

A playground was in front of the concessions building, which was "paneled with knotty pine and (an) asphalt tile floor." The ad promised that "the rest rooms are clean and sanitary and feature the most modern in fixtures."

The opening of the Tri-State came at a time when drive-ins were mushrooming across the American landscape. The post-war baby boom was in full swing, suburbs were expanding and Detroit was pumping out more and more Fairlanes, Belairs and Electras.

Drive-ins were thought to combine the best aspects of America's twin loves for movies and mobility. And rather than the contemporary perception of drive-ins as hormone-drenched "passion pits," they were marketed in the 1950s as an ideal destination for a family outing; Mom and Dad could watch the main features while the kids ate hot dogs and candy, played on the

---

Left: The screen for the Tri-State Drive-In is still visible when you drive along Rt. 18 in Slovan.

Above: The Tri-State Drive-In in Slovan has been closed since 1987.

Left: This Tri-State Drive-In ad ran Friday, July 1, 1955, in the Washington Reporter.

swing sets and fell asleep in the back of the station wagon. And when they made noise, they didn't bother anyone else.

It was also a time when people typically got dressed up to go to the movies. There was no need for that at the drive-in. You could come as you were. It was typical for young children to wear pajamas, since they were usually asleep by the second feature.

By 1958, there were 5,000 drive-ins in America; just 10 years before there were only 1,000.

"The drive-in was invented for families," said Susan Sanders, the co-author of the books "The American Drive-In Theater" and "Drive-In Movie Memories." "It didn't become a hang-out for teenagers until later."

Sanders also noted that drive-ins attracted many mom-and-pop investors. All you really needed was a little bit of land and a little bit of cash.

"You could build a drive-in for not a lot of money and make a lot of money," she said.

The Tri-State Drive-In was owned for 22 years by brothers Tony and Dominic Mungello. Tony's son, Anthony Mungello, explained that his father already ran the Maryann Theater in Burgettstown and the Penn Theater in Slovan, and opening a drive-in was a way to get more muscle when it came to dealing with film distributors.

"They were packing them in," he said. "The reason my father got in the drive-in theater business was necessity."

Sometimes films would shift from one theater to another; they would be shown at the drive-in, then go over to the Maryann or Penn theaters. Mungello was often the courier, shuttling the movies one or two reels at a time between the movie houses.

"We would start at the Maryann, and I would get a couple of reels and run them up to the drive-in, and then a couple more reels," said Mungello, who is now 64. "We kept going back and forth."

There's still a hint of pride in his voice when Mungello recounts what he believes made the Tri-State special: the pizza, the hamburgers, frozen candy and water drawn from an artesian well.

There are also special memories, like the time 15 kids were crammed into the trunk of a DeSoto. Or when they would screen movies from dusk until dawn.

Mungello is now retired after working at a Chrysler plant in Ohio for more than 30 years. He returned to Burgettstown, where many of his neighbors still have fond memories of trips to the Tri-State.

"I always thought that was one hell of a place," said Joseph Abate, an 86-year-old lifelong Burgettstown resident who was once a projectionist at the drive-in. "I just marveled at it. It was top of the trade."

Elsie Smith and her husband, Norman, would routinely pile their family into a car and make the brief trip to Slovan for a night out.

"It was really easy for us," she said. "The kids had a good time. There were things for them to do."

Business at the Tri-State tapered off through the 1960s and 1970s, as it did at most other drive-ins. Among the culprits were color television and daylight-saving time, which pushed back the starting time of the first feature at many theaters until at least 9 p.m.

Along the way, drive-ins ended up acquiring an unsavory reputation, especially when some started showing porn or Z-grade exploitation flicks. The Mungellos never went that route and neither did the late Bill Dugas Sr., the owner of Panhandle Food Sales, who purchased the drive-in in 1977.

Dugas originally bought the Tri-State with an eye toward expanding his own operation. However, he decided to keep it going just to see if he could spin a few more dollars out of it.

"We figured we would run it and see if it was viable," said his son, Bill Dugas Jr.

It stayed afloat for another decade. But by September 1987, the Dugases threw up the white flag, surrendering to demographic shifts and changing tastes. By the time it was shuttered, the Tri-State was typically drawing fewer than 25 patrons per show.

"Insurance started to go up," Dugas added. "It wasn't worth the manpower."

Just as the Tri-State arrived when drive-ins were in their heyday, it exited when they were precipitously declining. When the 1980s began there were about 3,500 drive-ins across the country. By the end of the decade, there were only about 1,000. Now, it's estimated there are roughly 800.

But when times were good, the Tri-State was a win-win for both its owners and its patrons. It was a convenient and affordable night of entertainment for local residents, and put food on the table for its owners.

"It was a good business," Mungello said. "We made a good living."

Above: Sign along Route 18 in Slovan.

A 30-Year Favorite

Published May 29, 2005
Hollywood Bar B-Q was a popular dining spot,
sadly missed when it closed.

By Kathie O. Warco, Staff writer

Apple, berry, cherry, peach, coconut cream and lemon meringue, chuckled Vivian Bales Harbison, rattling off the pies served daily.

Gone for more than 25 years, the Hollywood Bar B Q was the original gathering place in Peters Township at a time when more acreage was devoted to farmland than commercial ventures. The closing of the Hollywood on Feb. 22, 1979, was seen as a passing of history at Donaldsons Crossroads.

Harbison's dad, Henry "Charlie" Bales, her mom, Nina Bales, and his brother-in-law, Bernie Roth, purchased the restaurant from Bales' brother Irwin after World War II. The restaurant originally was at the corner of West McMurray Road and Route 19, at the current site of the CVS Pharmacy, before moving across the street and a few doors to the north on Route 19 in the mid-1950s.

"When I first saw those diamond-shaped windows, I thought back to the old Hollywood because it had the same shape windows," Harbison said. "It was like déja vu when I saw those."

Not surprisingly, barbecued meat was on the menu.

"They always had barbecue, that's how they got the name," Harbison said. "There was barbecue ham, beef and pork."

She had no idea where the Hollywood came from, but speculated it could have been her uncle's wishful thinking.

"When he sold the bar, he moved to California," she said.

Barbecue was not the only fare on the menu. Every day, there was a special, in addition to chicken, shrimp and steaks. French fries were especially crispy and hamburgers were made on the spot, not hurriedly thawed from the freezer. The meringue on the cream pies was piled high.

Harbison remembers her mother rising early each morning to bake the pies that were offered every day.

"I remember bugging her: 'Why can't we go here or why can't we go there,' and she'd always tell me that she had to get the pies done," Harbison said. "Finally, she got someone else trained to make the pies."

The atmosphere was friendly, not fancy. There was a counter with stools and booths near the front windows with little jukeboxes on each table. There were also tables in a back room and a large jukebox.

"We knew the regulars on a first-name basis," she said.

Left: Customers chat in one of the booths at the Hollywood Bar B-Q.

The Hollywood was her family's life. It was open for breakfast, lunch and dinner Monday through Saturday. On Sundays, a young Vivian would join her dad while he cleaned the restaurant for the next week. She was kept occupied by the coins he gave her to drop in the jukebox. The brothers-in-law would alternate shifts with one taking the day turn and the other handling the night duty and then switching off the following week, Harbison said.

"I can remember him buffing the floors," she said. "I probably drove him nuts."

The Hollywood was a gathering place for a variety of people, from businessmen in suits and horsemen talking equines to softball teams looking to quench their thirst or families in for a good meal. Legend has it that the bar was the scene of a snowball fight.

It was also where Jerry Harbison met his future bride. He and his dad would often go to the Hollywood for lunch, meeting the other regulars. He remembers some coming from Dormont after a day of golfing or fishing. Some of them would even show up and help them clean the place on Sundays.

"There were some characters," Jerry Harbison chuckled. "It was just a meeting place for everyone. I ate there every day. The food was great."

The salmon cakes were one of his personal favorites.

Jerry Harbison said his father-in-law served up not only good food to his customers but a helping hand.

"If anyone needed help, Charlie was always there for them," Harbison said. "He did so much good for his customers."

Dr. Howard Jack, who retired as superintendent of Peters Township School District 22 years ago, remembers the occasional Peters Township Chamber of Commerce meetings at the Hollywood.

"It was a very popular place," Jack recalled. "Bernie was quite the congenial host."

What Jack remembers best is the waitress who took 20 to 25 lunch orders from the members without writing anything down.

Robert Chamberlin, who owned Chamberlin Signs before retiring and moving to Ronks in Lancaster County, also remembers Ruth.

"She would take every order without writing anything down and when it came time to serve it, everyone got just what they ordered," Jack said. "Then when we got our bills, we were charged for what we ordered. Her memory was phenomenal."

"She would take all our orders and put everything down in front of the right person," Chamberlin said.

Chamberlin was one of the Hollywood regulars. The Hollywood has been the subject of the amateur oil painter's works.

"I lived in Peters for 50 years," Chamberlin said. "I always went to the Hollywood. The kitchen was exceptionally small, but the food was exceptionally good," he added. "I remember the days when you could get a barbecue sandwich for 35 cents and a good plate lunch for $1.25 with a slice of pie for a quarter."

Fridays were his favorite.

"I loved their shrimp and fries," Chamberlin said. "I'd often stop after work and get two orders to go and take it home. They also knew how to make spaghetti and had great roast beef," he added. "I was so disappointed when they closed."

Both Charlie and Bernie were good guys, he recalled.

Above: Chef's Restaurant, circa 1951, later became the second location of Hollywood Restaurant.

Above: Hollywood Bar B-Q's first location, where the current CVS has its parking lot.

Below: Bernie Roth tends the cash register at the Hollywood Bar B-Q.

"I took care of their neon signs," Chamberlin said. "When I did the work, Charlie couldn't wait to get the bill so he could pay it right away."

Dr. Jeffrey Mertens opened his dental practice 32 years ago, on Route 19 just a few doors down from the former spot of the Hollywood.

"It always drew a crowd with lots of locals," said Mertens. "It was really the only place to go in the late '60s and early '70s for a quick lunch.

Tom McCrory was only 4 or 5 years old when his dad, Mac McCrory, started taking him to the Hollywood.

"My dad probably paid for that building," laughed the Peters Township native. "The food was good. I was a hamburger-and-fries kind of kid.

"If we were on vacation, even if it was 12 hours away on the coast, Dad wouldn't stop to eat until he got back to the Hollywood," McCrory added.

As a youngster, he was impressed by one bartender's ability to tear telephone books in two.

McCrory remembers the picnics at Canonsburg Lake hosted each summer by the owners for the regulars.

Vivian Harbison's parents sold their interest in the restaurant to Roth in the early 1970s. Roth closed it when the lease for the building was not renewed.

"Everyone was so disappointed when it closed," Jack said. "It was a favorite spot for everyone. There weren't many good places to go, and we were fortunate to have a good one."

Above: The Hollywood Bar B-Q, circa 1977.

Left: Customers sip on Iron City draft beer on February 20, 1979, two days before the closing of the Hollywood Bar B-Q.

Wheeling & Main

Published February 22, 2004

Since the 1700s, the northeast corner of Wheeling and Main streets has been a vital part of Washington County history.

By Park Burroughs

At the northeast corner of Main and Wheeling streets in Washington stands a solid, three-story brick building. An antiques store and radio station WJPA occupy the first floor, and hundreds of people stream in an out of its basement every day for food and drink at the popular restaurant, the Union Grill.

But the greater part of this building – its top two floors – is empty, its windows boarded, its purpose and content a mystery to most. This was the William Henry Hotel until it closed in the mid-1950s. A hotel under one name or another had operated continuously on that site since 1791, making it the most hospitable corner in the city. The Union Grill's advertisements describe the bar and restaurant as the place "where friends meet." And they have, for well over two centuries and for longer than any other place in the city.

But this piece of ground was anything but hospitable in the city's earliest days. In the fall of 1782, William Darby came with his parents to the settlement then known as Bassett Town.

"The site where Washington now stands was a vast thicket of black and red hawthorn, wild plums, hazel bushes, scrub oak, and briars," he recalled in a newspaper article published in 1845. "Often I have picked hazel nuts where the courthouse now stands. The yell of the savage rung in fancy's ear and, alas, too often in the heart of the dying victim. The whole country was a dense forest, only broken by small patches, with dead trees, made so by the axe of the early pioneer."

Nine years later, Charles Valentine purchased the property at the northeast corner of what is now Wheeling and Main streets. Valentine built a log house on the plot, secured a license from the county court and opened it in the fall of 1791 as an inn and tavern called the White Goose. At the time there were probably no more than 400 residents in the town, which was renamed Washington in 1784.

John Rettig acquired the property in 1806 and renamed it the Golden Swan, but it was popularly referred to at the time as "the Sign of the Swan."

Birth of the Reporter

It was Rettig who entertained a pair of itinerant printers in the summer of 1808. William Brown and William Sample rode into Washington on a Conestoga wagon, hauling a hand-operated

Left: A view of South Main Street in 1875, looking north, shows the Valentine House on the right. It was a brick building measuring 60 feet by 180 feet. Built in 1846, it was destroyed by fire on Jan. 21, 1899.

printing press and supplies with which to start a newspaper and stopped for the night at the Swan. They had intentions of heading for Kentucky.

Earle R. Forrest, in his history of Washington County, wrote that Rettig sat on a bench with the two men, watching the sun set and imploring them to print a newspaper in Washington that could offer an opposing view to the federalist-leaning Western Telegraphe.

Rettig offered them the cellar of the building, and on Aug. 15, 1808, the first copy of The Reporter was printed in what is now the Union Grill.

The newspaper operated in the basement for about a year before moving on to other locations, and the tavern passed into the hands of Juliana Valentine in 1810.

John Valentine took over the business in 1819 and played host to the inn's most unusual guest: Columbus the elephant.

The elephant came to Washington on June 28, 1819, and was exhibited to the public at Valentine's Tavern. Admission was 25 cents for adults and half that amount for children. It was boarded in the stables behind the inn on Wheeling Street.

The inn had several other proprietors and names after that and was last called Washington Hall before the old buildings were torn down in 1846 and a three-story brick building erected. The new hotel was called Valentine House, which seemed appropriate as it had been in the hands of the Valentine family for so many years. The building was three stories and measured 60 by 180 feet. Like the present structure, it also housed several businesses on its basement and first-floor levels.

About 1880, the hotel was sold to M.M. Little, and by him to Jonathan Allison. Shortly after that, the name was changed to the Allison House.

"With the change in name there has also been a marked change in the character of the well known

Above: The Valentine House hotel, as it appeared in the 1870s.

Right: William Henry Hotel, Washington, PA circa 1920.

hostelry," read an article in a special business section of a local newspaper in 1896. "It is, however, a house of altogether a different kind to that which preceded it; it is a modern hotel in every respect, with every convenience that could be desired."

Above: A view looking down the second floor of the former William Henry Hotel located above WJPA radio station on the corner of South Main Street and Wheeling Street in Washington.

Below: Inside a bathroom of the William Henry Hotel, as it appears today.

The "character" of the hotel may have improved, but its proprietor at the time, J.C. Morrow, also operated a billiard saloon in its basement.

Destroyed By Fire

At 7:30 Saturday morning, Jan. 21, 1899, a grease fire in the kitchen of the hotel got out of control and spread to the rest of the building. All guests and employees escaped, but the building was destroyed. An article on the fire in The Washington Reporter two days later remarked: "Miss Effie, daughter of Armstead Skinner, pastry cook at Hotel Allison, lost all her clothing and $25 in money, which she had saved to pay on her piano. She intended making a payment to-day, and takes her loss very hard."

Simon Siegel, who owned the building, constructed a new three-story hotel on the property and opened it as the Siegel House in 1903, the same year the Washington Trust Building was finished.

According to his grandson, Michael Siegel, owner of radio station WJPA with offices and studio on the first floor of the building, Simon Siegel was a Russian immigrant who worked as a peddler before acquiring wealth as a clothing merchant and in real estate.

Simon Siegel also built another structure along East Wheeling Street, and today the Siegel family still owns the buildings.

As was the case with the old Valentine House, the top floors were all guest rooms and most of the basement and first floor of the new building were

Above: The main stairway of the William Henry Hotel is an impressive display of elaborate woodwork.

occupied by various businesses. Where WJPA is now was at various times a clothing store, pharmacy and restaurant. From 1956 until 1968, when the radio station moved there from the George Washington Hotel, Becker's Boot Shop did business there.

The space that is now Downtown Antiques was previously Ace Auto and Sporting Goods. Directly beneath it, where the Union Grill's banquet room is now, was a bowling alley and pool hall in the early 1900s, according to Lee and Sue Allen, who own Downtown Antiques.

William Henry Hotel Recalled

The name of the hotel was changed to the William Henry Hotel in 1919 by its new proprietor, William Henry Lippincott, of Waynesburg. It operated under that name until it closed in the mid-1950s.

Charles Waychoff worked at the William Henry Hotel from 1948 to 1950 when he was a student at Trinity High School.

"I started out as a bell hop and later became the night desk clerk on weekends," Waychoff said from his home in Tampa, Fla. "There were about 20 to 25 rooms on each floor, and there was a restaurant where the radio station is now - the Rose Grill - and my mother ran it."

Waychoff recalled that the William Henry was taken over by the Army for two years during the war to house soldiers being trained at Washington & Jefferson College.

When he worked there, "it was pretty decent for a cheap hotel. The guests were mostly transient - working people who couldn't afford the George Washington Hotel."

Today, the windows are all boarded and the wide corridors are cold and dark. Green paint peels from the walls and ceilings and dust carpets the floors, but the walnut woodwork is still in place, as are solid-wood doors, marble sinks and enameled, cast-iron bath tubs with claw feet. "There have been times, like when snow was on the satellite dish on the roof, that I would have to go upstairs," said Bob Gregg, operations director for WJPA. "It's dark, it's been unoccupied for 60 years, but you'd hear a noise - plaster falling or something - and think, 'What is that?' It's kind of creepy."

Michael Siegel said he has been asked to sell the woodwork and fixtures but has refused. Although the cost of refurbishing the upper floors could be prohibitive, he has not completely ruled it out.

The Union Grill began as the Venice Beer Garden, opened by Peter Celani and Dominick and Louis Aloia in about 1935. They sold the business to John Valitutti and Carmen Nicolella in 1939, and they gave it its current name, "because of the stone masons - union workers - who used to hang out here," according to Michael Flynn, who bought the business in 1967.

The hotel that Simon Siegel built has stood on the northeast corner of Wheeling and Main for more than 100 years, and far longer than any other in its place. It was solidly constructed and remains so. With any luck, it will remain there for many years to come, a reminder – like the courthouse and the Trust Building – of the city's greater past, of its golden era of prosperity and optimism.

Sources: Forrest, Earle. History of Washington County, Pa. (S.J. Clarke Publishing Co., Chicago, 1926)

Knestrick, Ray. Old Buildings on Main Street, Washington, Pa. (Lydic Printing Co., Washington, Pa., 1975)

McFarland, Joseph F. 20th Century History of the City of Washington and Washington County. (Richmond-Arnold Publishin Co., Chicago, 1910)

The Reporter, Washington, Pa. Jan. 23, 1899; Aug. 15, 1958.

The Washington Weekly Democrat. Special Business Edition, December 1897.

Right: The old William Henry Hotel circa 2004 on the corner of South Main Street and Wheeling Street in Washington. An antiques store and WJPA radio station occupy the first floor and the Union Grill is in the basement. The top two floors are now empty.

The Twin Coaches

Published January 8, 2006
*This Mon Valley supper club wowed audiences of the '50s and '60s in
the heyday of live entertainment in nightclubs.*

By Scott Beveridge

Sammy Davis Jr. did not set the house on fire the last time he was booked at a once-famous Mon Valley supper club.

That's because his appearance was canceled by a second mysterious blaze within hours that destroyed the Twin Coaches on the first day of Fire Prevention Week in October 1977.

"I remember it like it was yesterday," said Mike Godzak, 46, of Rostraver Township, who was among the first firefighters on scene when the fire was burning out of control.

Godzak said he and others "scrambled off the roof" as it was collapsing into the ballroom, and were fortunate to avoid injury.

Hours earlier, they had doused a small fire among linens stored too close to a hot water tank. Embers from the second blaze smoldered for a week at the Westmoreland County business. The damage was so severe that it apparently prevented investigators from determining the cause of the blaze that brought down the curtain on one of the most famous stages east of the Mississippi River.

"It was 35 miles from the big city and it was packed all the time. That was the beauty of it," said Cassandra Vivian, chief executive officer of Monessen Heritage Museum, recalling the nightclub where every big name in the 1950s and 1960s except for Frank Sinatra had wooed audiences.

Meanwhile, crooner Bobby Vinton was a big draw, even before his signature song, "Roses are Red," shot up the charts in 1962.

"It was one of the highlights of my early career," Vinton said in a telephone interview.

The Canonsburg native was often in the audience as a fan while studying music at Duquense University in Pittsburgh.

His favorite memory there was meeting John F. Kennedy and his wife, Jackie, in 1959 during the then-Massachusetts senator's campaign for the White House.

"He shook my hand and said, 'Hello.' Here I was, just a young kid from Canonsburg," the 70-year-old Vinton said.

The club's owner at the time, Rose Calderone, wanted to give the Kennedys the royal treatment, and instructed her kitchen staff to prepare them lobster. It was a Friday and the future Roman Catholic president could not dine on steak for religious reasons, said Ron Paglia, a former newspaper editor in the Mon Valley.

"He said, 'No, Rose. Give me some scrambled eggs and a beer,'" Paglia said.

Calderone ushered Kennedy to her private kitchen, seated

Left: The Eddy Warren Band performed at the Twin Coaches in the early 1960s.

him on a stepstool and served him eggs and a bottle of Stoney's, a local label produced in Smithton by the family of actress Shirley Jones.

Kennedy was not the only big-name politician to visit the Calderones. President Harry Truman, the nation's 33rd president, gave a speech at their club in the 1950s.

Calderone and her husband, Tony, had purchased what was a run-down bar in need of a more-refined clientele in the 1940s. He had taken a gamble on what amounted to two rusting Pullman railroad cars parked side-by-side, the 91-year-old Rostraver Township woman said, discussing her

Above: Canonsburg native Bobby Vinton appeared at the Twin Coaches before and after his first hit recording, "Roses are Red."

famous career in October at her kitchen table.

She said she stood at the bar's front door and barred men from entering if they were not wearing a coat and tie. She kept a baseball bat behind the bar in case of trouble.

In 1950, her husband added the 250-seat Rose Room to the establishment and booked television celebrity Al Morgan to perform.

"He had vision. He really did," Calderone said of her husband.

Three years later, he built the Butterfly Room, adding 1,000 seats to the club, making it the largest nightclub in the Pittsburgh region. Pop singer Tony Martin opened the room with four black-lit butterflies on its ceiling, along with Alan King, his warm-up comic.

"It just grew, and Rose came along, and she booked the best," said Warren Sheppick of Fallowfield Township, who played tenor saxophone in the house band. "It was the place to play."

Sheppick said he performed for Liberace, the Four Tops, Diana Ross and the Supremes, Johnny Mathis and Rosemary Clooney.

"They had all the big names," Paglia added.

Rose Calderone took center stage when her husband died unexpectedly in 1960.

Above: Monessen Mayor Hugo Parenti, left; Rose Calderone, wife of Twin Coaches owner Tony Calderone; singer Johnny Mathis; Adeline Parenti, wife of the mayor; and Calderone are pictured at the Twin Coaches.

"It was either sink or swim," she said. She befriended the stars and traveled to New York or Las Vegas to haggle with the top booking agents.

Her hard work also provided well-paying jobs for women who lived in the small coal towns that dotted the region.

"Some of the waitresses, ladies in the 1950s, were making $100 a night in tips. That was good money then," Vivian said.

The club was on the national radar screen because guests on the Tonight Show often mentioned it when host Johnny Carson asked them where they would be performing, Vivian said. Calderone was even profiled in 1969 in

Above: Among the really notable visitors were Smithton native Shirley Jones and her husband, Jack Cassidy, who dined at the Twin Coaches.

Left: Pennsylvania Gov. William Scranton speaks at the Twin Coaches.

Below: A promotional photo of Sonny and Cher was used for a Twin Coaches appearance.

Cosmopolitan magazine because of her Hollywood friends and success in the male-dominated show business.

She later sold her club to a group of investors, not long after supper clubs were losing their popularity, and she had converted hers into a dinner theater. She decided to invest in a Holiday Inn across the highway.

The nation's nightclub trade began to die with the arrival of the Beatles in February 1964, Vinton said.

Rock and roll demanded much-larger concert halls, the size of which, Calderone said, she could not compete against.

"Entertainment changed," Vinton said.

"The time was up for the big supper clubs," he said. "You had TV. People didn't go as much ...."

Really 'Old Hat'

Published June 26, 2005
Time was when hats were 'de rigueur' for gentlemen, these days hats are a bit, well...

By Joe Tuscano

A few years before women began burning their bras and teenagers torched their draft cards, another revolt spread across the country in a quieter manner.

When newly elected President John F. Kennedy invited the American people to ask what they could do for their country, they responded in mass by removing their hats, just as Kennedy did at the 1960 presidential inauguration.

Women still kept the tradition, needing them for social occasions, church and other functions. Today, however, even that fashion statement has faded.

"In my day, you just weren't dressed up unless you had a hat on," said Al Sauter, 97, who lives in Westminster Place at Presbyterian Senior Care in Washington.

"Theaters, shows, restaurants, ice cream parlors, you name it. Most men wore hats when they went there. At one time, hats were everywhere," Sauter said. "Now, they wear ballcaps."

When Ken Harvey left the Army following World War II, he couldn't wait to enjoy the simple pleasures found in his hometown of Wellsburg, W.Va.

After being discharged from the Army, where he served as commander of a half-track in the 2nd Infantry Division, Harvey initially pursued the rewards of home life, including a soft bed, the renewal of friendships and a good meal.

When Harvey began courting Marjorie Sayer in 1947, he needed a hat. So he stopped into one of the local hat shops along the main street and picked out a straw hat, tightly woven with a stiff brim.

"We wore them to special events," Harvey said. "We felt a hat was for special occasions. A lot of people used to wear pins in their hats, political pins and what-not. I would cut the brim with a pair of scissors to make it shorter, but there were a lot of people who wore the wide-brimmed hats, especially for church."

Harvey, now 84 and retired from his last job as a sales representative for the Pettibone Corp. in Bethel Park, has three of his favorites hats stored in the closet. Greek fishermen hats, two black and one brown, that were popular in the early '60s, are his pride and joy now.

"Everyone wants to know where I got them," he said.

Most of the time, he smiles but won't tell them he picked them up at an outlet store in Myrtle Beach, S.C.

When Sauter needed a hat, he usually found what he was

Left: Newsboys for The Reporter play marbles in 1918.

looking for on the main streets of Washington. Like Harvey, Sauter had a preference for the short-brimmed straw hat that could be purchased for a few dollars.

"Some of the straw hats were more pliable but most of them were real hard," said Sauter, who ran Sauter's Garage on Banksville Road in Pittsburgh for 50 years, until his retirement in the late '70s.

"Felt hats came in a box but straw hats were normally set out on hangers. You weren't dressed up unless you had a hat on."

Two stores in Washington, the Capital Hat Shop at 30 North Main St. and the Paris Hat Shop two blocks down, were popular as was Madge Dugan's Hat Shop in the Washington Trust Building.

Many of the stores that sold hats also serviced them by offering cleaning. But many shoe-shine stands also offered the service. A hat would be "blocked" or placed on a round piece of wood that would support it while being cleaned. Steam was used to remove tough stains and winkles in the material.

"Some of the hat stores were located in these long, skinny buildings," Harvey said. "The shoe-shine places weren't very large but you could have your hat cleaned while your shoes were being shined."

Hats have been around for most of history, the earliest record coming from the drawings on cave walls that showed primitive man wearing what appeared to

Above: Two unidentified gentlemen, circa 1920.

Left: A band, circa 1870, poses for a photo before a parade in Washington.

be a head covering, probably of animal skin.

Over the years, hats have been redesigned, reshaped and reconfigured to fit the times. From the capotain, sugar loaf and tri-cornered hats of the 17th century to the more modern top hat and Panama hat, made from the toquilla plant, to today's baseball caps, hats have always been a popular piece of our wardrobe.

"I used to have a felt hat but it was really too dressy for me," said Sauter. "Richer men in the community wore felt hats."

Not wearing a hat in the '30s and '40s was a sign of independence, Bill Mathewson felt. The 81-year-old retiree rarely wore one during his 35-year career as a children's photographer in Mt. Lebanon.

"I only put one on when it was raining," he said.

His choice was a softer felt hat that had a wider brim. He purchased them in much the same way others did, through one of the major retailers.

"It cost less," Mathewson said.

Most places provided hat stands, hat hooks or a hat-check area so men would not have to hold them while in public.

Many homes had specific places to hang hats, from the standard hat stand to the more impressive versions that included an attached mirror and bench seat that lifted so coats and scarfs could be stored. The bench could also be used when putting on shoes or snow boots.

"What I thought was interesting about those times is that no one ever stole your hat if you left it hanging somewhere," Harvey said. "It's not like today; you couldn't do that."

Above: Former Gov. Edward Martin chats with a friend in his hometown of Ten Mile in the late 1950s.

Left: Most of the carriers for The Reporter wore hats in 1918. These boys carried the noon edition of the newspaper, which also came out with a 3:30 p.m. edition.

97

Harness Veteran

Joseph M. McGraw of Washington is a veteran starter and judge of harness racing. For over 60 years he has been active in the sport at tracks throughout the nation. During this time McGraw has introduced many new developments to harness racing which have made it a better sport and one which is growing in interest today. A testimonial dinner in McGraw's honor in 1957 was a feature of the first Arden Downs Stakes races which were introduced by Del Miller.

Above: Straw boaters and top hats were the favorites of the Washington & Jefferson College class of 1885.

Left: Clipping from the Aug. 8, 1958 edition of The Washington Reporter.

Right: At the City of Washington's sesquicentennial celebration in 1960: from left, Col. Lawrence Stewart, Pennsylvania National Guard; Jack Merdian, WJPA general manager; and Washington Mayor George Krause.

Day at the Beach

Published August 1, 2004
Willow Beach in Houston is long gone, but memories of its
versatile character linger on.

By David Penn

Willow Beach Park in Houston had a little something for everyone: picnicking, dancing and boating, as well as boxing in a ring at the center of a man-made lake.

Today, there's no sign that the park ever existed. Driving along Western Avenue out of Houston, it is hard to imagine hundreds of people converging on the other side of Little Chartiers Creek to while away summer days dancing, swimming and roller skating. American Legion Post 902 now owns nearly all of the land where Willow Beach stood during the middle part of the 1900s.

Among the earliest examples of a public recreation spot in Washington County, Willow Beach emerged from the inspiration of a coal miner turned entrepreneur, Simeon Cornelius Reynolds. Born in England in 1878, Reynolds came to the United States with his mother and siblings shortly before his 11th birthday. His father had come to Mercer County in Pennsylvania some years earlier to work in the coal mines and save money for his family's passage to America.

According to an incomplete memoir that's been photocopied and passed among his descendants, Reynolds received no formal schooling after he left England. His older brother Will, then 14, went to work in the mine with their father within weeks of settling in Pennsylvania, and Sim followed soon after. The family moved intermittently, following work, and at various times lived in Castle Shannon, Grove City and Leechburg.

Reynolds was a miner for much of his young life. But, inspired in part by Will, the family's letter writer, he practiced reading and writing and took correspondence courses with the aim of becoming a fire boss, foreman and, later, inspector, in the intervening years working in mines in Ellsworth and Canonsburg, among others. He eventually became an inspector for Aetna, by which time he had married his wife, Mary, and had several children.

Reynolds leased the land that would become Willow Beach in 1922. According to research conducted by Canonsburg historian James T. Herron Jr., Reynolds hired out teams of horses and men to cut a channel across a bend in the creek to form the lake where once there had been only a private swimming hole, and built a complementary pool measuring 500 feet long. He opened the park to the public on July 4, 1922.

Left: About to take a ride are, from left, Wayne McDaniel, Mildre Reynolds, Margaret Reynolds and Mary Reynolds Donaldson.

But, as Herron notes, swimming alone wasn't going to make the park a success. A two-story pavilion with an oak dance floor, combined with burgeoning public interest in jazz, would keep Willow Beach in the black and in the newspapers. It was a winning idea, but where exactly Reynolds got his inspiration for the park is uncertain.

Above: Simeon Cornelius Reynolds, seated next to his wife, Mary, built Willow Beach Park after spending much of his young life working in coal mines.

"I have no idea why he decided to do that, but it turned out to be a heck of a place," said Thomas Reynolds, Simeon and Mary Reynolds' youngest son, now 81 years old and living in Fresno, Calif.

Thomas Reynolds spent his childhood in the park. He said many people rented boats to go fishing or just enjoy an afternoon on the lake, which ran as deep as eight feet and eventually took in several acres. You could rent bathing suits, as well. Included in the dime rental fee were wicker baskets to carry clothing and numbered slugs patrons pinned to their suits.

A reliable water supply came from an artesian well tapped into an underground waterway. The well was so productive, in fact, that it supplied water to Canonsburg Borough during a drought, Reynolds said.

Refreshment stands offered ice cream and root beer. On holidays, contestants vied to catch greased pigs and climb greased poles. People swam out to the center of the lake to watch boxing matches in an island ring, and musicians sometimes played on a nearby platform.

Above: Patrons could rent swimsuits at the lake. Each was assigned a numbered slug that was pinned to the suit.

"There used to be two or three thousand people there at a time. That was no problem at all on a busy day," said Reynolds.

Success had its pitfalls, though. Almost immediately after the park opened, local church leaders tried to stop Willow Beach from doing business on Sundays, a matter fought out first in the pages of the Canonsburg Daily Notes, then in court. Dancing, not swimming on the Sabbath, was the likely source of the contention, given the unquestioned Sunday business at Linden Beach in nearby North Strabane Township.

In an outline of his unfinished memoir, Simeon Reynolds describes the end of the face-off tersely: "Litigation with Blue Law enthusiasts 1926-1927 to keep park open on 'Lord's Day.' Estimated cost $10,000. Won. Built 3rd Street home."

The house on Third Street in Houston still stands, though it is no longer in the family. One of several houses Reynolds built at the park remains, as well. Reynolds' grandson, David Warne of South Franklin Township, owns it.

Reynolds "built these cottages to rent them out. He was one of those people who never sits still. He was always coming up with something new," said Warne.

After Willow Beach was established, Reynolds began developing a property outside Morgantown, W.Va., that became Riverside Park, an equal

success. While determination had raised Reynolds up from poverty, however, very little could have protected him from the danger looming ahead.

The Great Depression brought to a close the first chapter of Willow Beach's history. With massive unemployment, there simply weren't enough customers to make the business profitable. Again in the outline of his memoir, Reynolds notes returning to work as a mine safety engineer in Canonsburg between 1935 and 1940 in order to survive. He would make a go of Riverside Park again in the 1940s, but gave up managing Willow Beach.

When Willow Beach reopened on Memorial Day in 1939, a newspaper advertisement published the day before boasted new diving towers, new playground equipment and a half-mile bicycle path. Available historical resources on the park, however, give an incomplete picture of the park's management in the second half of its existence, and it appears to have closed and reopened on more than one occasion.

In "Houston, Then and Now," a book written by Felicia Browell in commemoration of the borough's

Above: Eight of the 15 children of Jim and Mary Reynolds pose for a photo in 1915.

centennial in 2001, the proceeding years are described succinctly:

"In 1940, Willow Beach was purchased by the Falconi interests. A few years later, Howard Metz Sr. owned and operated a popular roller skating rink there, and held Sunday night dances upstairs; this continued at least through 1970. In December 1972, the old pavilion and dance hall burned down."

An article about the history of Kennywood Park published in the Observer-Reporter in 1995 notes peripherally that Willow Beach Park closed in 1948. The lake itself existed at least until the early 1950s, as a Daily Notes article from February 1951 records the rescue of a child who had fallen through ice on the lake.

Above: People swam out to a ring in the middle of the lake to watch boxing matches, Musicians sometimes performed on the diving platform directly behind the ring.

Brief newspaper articles published following the 1972 fire note the pavilion was subject to frequent vandalism by that time, and the American Legion had been planning to convert the site to a picnic area. The cause of the fire isn't explained in the articles.

Later, in 1983, the spot attracted the attention of the Department of Energy, which had declared the former site of Vitro Manufacturing Co. in nearby Canonsburg a federal Superfund site. Radium and uranium extraction had occurred at the Canonsburg site starting in 1911 when the Standard Chemical Co. was located there, and, between 1942 and 1957, workers at Vitro processed uranium from waste generated at other weapons plants.

Again, men dug up vast swathes of earth in Houston, this time with motorized equipment. Long after the last swimmers had left Willow Beach, federal inspectors went there in search of the contaminated sand that had been trucked in from Canonsburg to fill its shores.

Memories of Willow Beach remain for many people who grew up in the Houston area, and several are working to keep them alive for at least a little while longer. The American Legion post recently hosted a successful "Willow Beach Reunion" with famed Pittsburgh disc jockey Porky Chedwick spinning the rock-and-roll-records he had played on the site decades earlier. Organizers at the post are looking to put together at least one more such reunion in the coming months.

Above: Patrons drink from a fountain at the lake. Water was supplied to the park by an artesian well tapped into the underground river.

Right: A view of Willow Beach Park in Houston with homes on a hill in Canonsburg in the background.

Below: Two signs, one strung across West Pike Street in Houston, point the way to Willow Beach Park.

A Traveler's Best Friend

Published February 26, 2006
There was a time when Waynesburg was the place to stay,
and the choices were many.

By Jon Stevens

Nearly 81 years have passed since the icy winds of a near-zero night swept through Waynesburg in the predawn hours of Dec. 23, 1925, compounding a tragedy that would change High Street forever.

Fire broke out in downtown Waynesburg, destroying three buildings - the Downey House, the Presbyterian Church on Church Street and the Grossman Building - and in the process, taking the lives of five volunteer firemen.

Two years later, the Fort Jackson Hotel, like the Phoenix rising out of the ashes, was built on the site of the Downey House on the corner of High and Washington streets, joining a family of establishments that dotted the skyline of Waynesburg from the Civil War to the end of World War II.

Fortunately, there have been people like the late John O'Hara, who embraced life through fact and folklore so that his readers would always remember when a fire nearly destroyed a town.

Left: The Messenger Building, better known as the Hamilton Hotel, stood at the corner of High and Washington streets.

And there is Dr. G. Wayne Smith, who has chronicled so much Greene County history that those who wish can, too, remember when people sat in sofas in hotel lobbies with a distant expression, valises at their side, and remember a bellman appearing when there was a ding!

There always has been something fascinating about hotels. Perhaps like those who frequented the Downey House barber shop before it was rendered to rubble, and took with them the memories of the barber shop's lure: "If you're wise, U R next. Six chairs. Six artists."

Or what of the wayward traveler, looking for a place to rest a weary body for the night, coming across the advertisement for the Walton House built in 1860. "I'll take care of you," Ned Walton, proprietor, promised. "This hotel has been renovated and greatly improved throughout; new furniture, toilet and bathrooms. It is furnished with the latest system of call bells, electric lights, and natural gas. You are cordially invited to call at the corner of Main (High) and Morris streets."

People who frequented the hotels in Waynesburg, and there were many to visit, were not from Waynesburg. It would have been easy to wonder who they were. What were their missions? Where had they come from?

No doubt, though, the truth was prosaic. Probably, they were salesmen or servicemen.

The Way Things Were

When the Downey House was built in 1869, it had some formidable competition for customers. There was, of course, the Walton Hotel, which had the renovated toilets. But the Downey House was not to be outdone in its flowery propaganda.

A newspaper advertisement claimed, "Persons who have put up at this Hotel will all testify that there is not a better arranged house or better accommodations anywhere."

Moreover, in a twist of irony, Edward B. (Ned) Walton, yes, of Walton House, served as one of the managers of Downey House.

Audrey Huffman of Waynesburg, a stately white-haired lady who has a thirst for her hometown hotel history, provided this insight into the Downey House lure.

She quoted G. Wayne Smith, who had noted in his "History of Greene County Pennsylvania," that the Downey House had 40 "splendidly furnished rooms, all carpeted, well heated" and lighted, several of which had private baths. There was an electric bell system and on the first floor there were two "handsomely furnished parlors and a "gentleman's writing room."

Huffman, who is the proprietor of the Corner Shoppe at 52 E. High St., said unabashedly, "There are not too many of us left who can remember these histories," she said.

Coincidentally, a place called Robert Cather's Inn, built in 1811, once stood where her shop now stands.

Ewing Pollock, a longtime Waynesburg attorney, who was recently honored by the Waynesburg Chamber of Commerce with its Distinguished Service Award, said, "Hotels back in the 1920s and 1930s were just the way things were. People traveling through had to have some place to sleep," he said.

Above: Edward B. "Ned" Walton managed the Walton Hotel, Downey House and Blair Hotel. A tuba player, he subsequently left Waynesburg to tour with a marching band playing a Sousaphone.

Pollock remembers quite well the Fort Jackson Hotel, considering it did not cease being a hotel until the late 1960s.

"It was built after the fire, so of course it was advertised as a fire-proof hotel,"

Pollock remembers the Walton Hotel, which was razed in 1945 but said he was never in it.

"I guess it would be safe to call the Fort Jackson Hotel the crown jewel, the centerpiece of hotels, in Waynesburg," Pollock said.

Above: The Walton Hotel was built in 1861 as a tavern and was razed in May 1945. It has occupied the northwest corner of West High and Morris streets in Waynesburg.

Banquets and Balls

More than 200 people from Waynesburg, Washington, Uniontown and Pittsburgh attended the opening reception and banquet of the new Fort Jackson Hotel.

The menu included melon cocktail, stuffed celery, olives, radishes, salted nuts, bisque of celery aux crouton, sweetbread patties, roast squab a la chipolata, pineapple ice, new potatoes Parisienne, Fort Jackson salad, French pastry, Silver King fizz, cigars and cigarettes.

The cost to build the hotel was $500,000. A newspaper account of the opening of the hotel, which was described as "one of the finest hotels in this part of the state," boasted that the hotel's prices have been fixed at $2 and $3.50 and that the management plans to give special attention to weekend parties.

Moreover, weekend guests will be given golf privileges at Greene County Country Club.

The newspaper goes on to say the three-story building houses seven business rooms in addition to the lobby on the first floor, and the second and third floors are devoted exclusively to hotel use and contain 70 guest rooms.

Over the course of time, the hotel became popular for social functions and a number of banquets, luncheons and dances.

During the first week the hotel was open five banquets and luncheons were served. The staff of the Waynesburg Hospital held a benefit dance and the Chamber of Commence and Kiwanis held luncheons.

"It was the social place to be," Huffman said.

But like the other fine hotels of Waynesburg, time won out over Fort Jackson.

In 1975, two Waynesburg residents purchased Fort Jackson and planned to continue to use it as an office and commercial building.

Five years earlier, Global Development of Washington purchased the building from Fort Jackson Hotel Co., several years after the hotel had been closed. Then in 1996, the Greene County commissioners bought the building for $265,000, less than half of what it cost to build the opulent hotel almost 70 years earlier.

Below: The Downey House barbershop, the best place to get a quick shave, and the quickest place to get the best shave.

Above: The Downey House Hotel, built in 1869, was consumed by fire in 1925.

Above: The Green House was for many years a hotel and barroom. Girls were taught classes on the second floor of the building in 1850 for what became the Female Department of Waynesburg College. The building is now occupied by Walton Financial, Catholic Charities and Padgett Business Services.

Left: The Messenger Building as it appears today.

Right: The Fort Jackson Building was a stately hotel when it was built in 1927. It served guests until closing in the late 1960s and now serves as an office building for Greene County government.

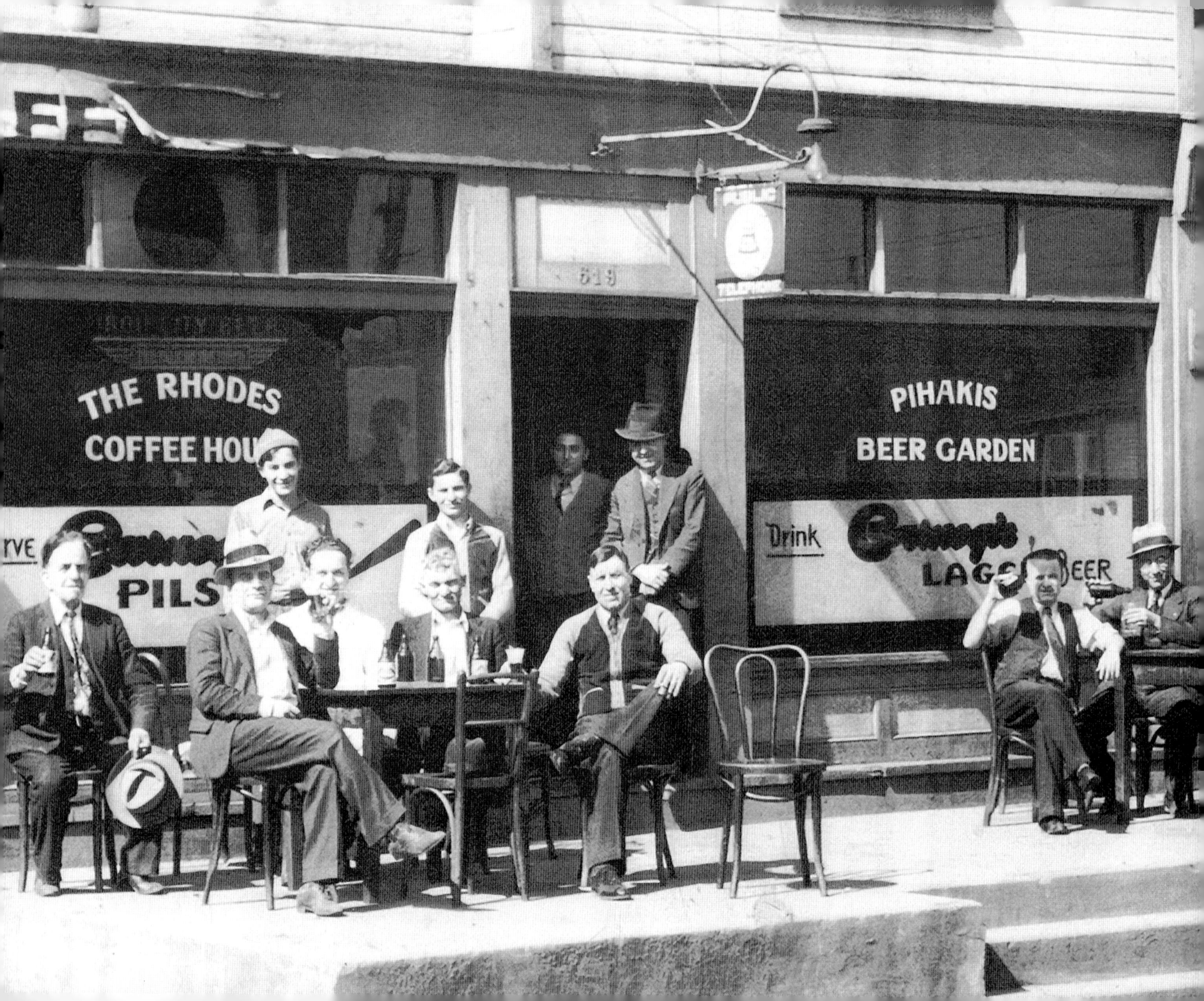
THE RHODES
COFFEE HOU
PIHAKIS
BEER GARDEN
PILS
Drink

The Heart of Town

Published March 21, 2004
Pihakis' Coffeehouse served as the anchor for
Canonsburg's Greek community.

By David Penn

On a bright summer day back in the 1970s, Frank Sarris remembers, a long, black limousine pulled up in front of his candy store on Adams Avenue in Canonsburg. Inside the limo was Perry Como, a Canonsburg barber who had gone on to become one of the world's best-known singers.

"He asked me, 'Where's Mr. Pihakis?'" Sarris said recently.

Michael Pihakis came strolling down the street not long after, on his daily walk uptown. Dressed in a neat button-down shirt with bright- green sports jacket, he was easy to spot, Sarris said. Como greeted Pihakis, shook his hand and took the elderly man on a tour of the borough in his limousine.

The gesture was well-appreciated, and appropriate. Fifty years earlier, Pihakis had given Como a barber shop.

"The old guy Perry worked for had died, so Mike just turned

Left: Seated outside Pihakis' building are a coterie of Pihakis' friends and acquaintances enjoying outdoor ambience and camaraderie. From left, seated, are Nick Kusturiss, William Eleamos, Steve Lemonakis, Nick Pihakis and George Frunja; standing are two sons of William Eleamos and Bill Pihiou. The photo was taken in the early 1930s. The gentlemen at the right are unidentified.

over the building to Perry. I think (Como) was about 14 years old," Sarris said.

By the time he took his first limousine ride, Pihakis was a grand old man of Canonsburg's close-knit East End neighborhood. He never owned his own car, but for nearly half a century his traditional Greek coffeehouse served as the center of the borough's Hellenic community. People socialized there, politicians stumped for votes there and the Orthodox Patriarch of Istanbul, Turkey, once hosted a church service there.

"We had weddings and baptisms in the coffeehouse. They held church services there before there was a Greek Orthodox church in Canonsburg," said Manuel Pihakis, a son of the late Michael Pihakis who remains active in the community and the church. "And on Friday and Saturday, it was a glendi; it was a party. All the Greek families came. There was singing and dancing, and it was a band, not a jukebox."

Como's barber shop was inside the building, to the right of the main entrance. Before Greek Orthodox weddings, Pihakis said, it was a custom for the groom to make a trip to the barber; the wedding party sang during the haircut, and tipped the young Como handsomely.

"People gave gold pieces: 5-dollar, 10-dollar coins. He could make three months' wages in one day," said Pihakis.

The elder Pihakis had come to the United States from the

Greek island of Rhodes in the early 1910s. He was single when he began working at the now-defunct Standard Plate & Tin, and he saved his money, according to his son. He built the three-floor coffeehouse in 1922, and soon accepted boarders in the building's 42 rooms. It stood next to Apollo Grocery between Blaine and Adams avenues until the 1970s.

It was open seven days a week, and the front door usually was unlocked.

"I don't think Mike P. even had a key to the place," said Sarris.

Each evening, men would return home from work, clean up, have dinner, then go out for coffee and cards. Imported Turkish coffee was brewed over heated sand in a small kettle known as cezve, then served in a demitasse about the size of an espresso cup. Card players favored pinochle and pastra while others played tavli, a Greek variant of backgammon.

Arguing was a popular pastime, too, said Sarris.

"People would fight with words. It was like a game; it worked out tensions," he said.

In short, the coffeehouse was a reproduction of the establishments the men had known at home, in Europe. Many who moved to Canonsburg from Greece lived in Pihakis' building until they could earn enough money to bring over their families and buy their own homes.

"He let people stay there for free," Pihakis said of his father. "Just about everyone who came over from Greece lived in the coffeehouse at first. It was almost like a little Ellis Island in Canonsburg."

As a child, Jim Gregorakis of Canonsburg played in the street outside the coffeehouse during the summer, while the older men sat on chairs nearby, enjoying the weather. He says his father, George, was one of the people who benefited from Pihakis's generosity.

Gregorakis' father was from Kremasti, a village on Rhodes. As the family story goes, a letter arrived in Kremasti saying there was work in Canonsburg, and 32 young men departed on a monthlong voyage to Southwestern Pennsylvania, George Gregorakis among them.

After getting off the train from Pittsburgh, the men walked the borough streets as a group, speaking only a few words of English and carrying all their belongings in knapsacks on their backs. They ran into Tom Vlachos, the owner of a candy store, who gave them directions to Pihakis' place.

"Mr. Pihakis put them up. The next day, most of them had jobs at Standard Plate & Tin," said Gregorakis, whose father was the last of the group to die, in 2000, at the age of 107.

It was a measure of Pihakis' standing in the community that 30 men just off the boat from Europe found work so quickly. While he lacked a formal education, he spoke the formal Greek of the church, and was able to communicate with the most influential people in the community.

"He wasn't a wealthy man, but he was a powerful man," said Sarris.

Gregorakis, himself a member of the recently reunited singing group the Four Coins, said his father and uncle played in a musical combo at the coffeehouse for many years. The house didn't pay them to play, but patrons dropped dollars for them in a box.

On Friday nights, whole families came, the women in patterned dresses, the men wearing clean, white shirts and straw hats. In the basement were a boxing ring and wrestling mat for the younger men, Pihakis' sons among them. Cooks were brought in for the weekend to make lamb shish kebab and "Greek" hamburgers, deep-fried patties made with ground beef, tomato, basil and chopped onion.

While other coffee shops popped up after Pihakis opened his, none of them achieved its stature in the community. When he finally retired, nothing like it would replace it. The younger generation didn't continue the business, which their father had run more or less by himself.

Manuel Pihakis had the building torn down in 1976. An apartment building stands on the spot now.

"A lot of that spirit is still in Canonsburg, though," said Pihakis, noting the Greek school operated by All Saints Greek Orthodox Church that teaches the language and culture to both children and adults.

And, while the coffee usually comes in Styrofoam cups, you still can get shish kebab or a Greek hamburger at the Greek food festival hosted by the church each summer.

Right: Pihakis' coffeehouse, Canonsburg, as it appeared in the early 1950s.

The Heart of Town

History on the Hill

Published April 18, 2004
Since 1853, Washington Cemetery has become
harbor to more than 44,000 souls.

By Byron Smialek

Just how many people are buried in Washington Cemetery? More than you might think.

From 1994 through 1997, when Quicksilver Golf Club in Midway was host to Senior PGA Tour events, it was speculated that the final day attendance - estimated at as many as 18,000 if the play was spectacular - would make the golf course the single most populated place in Washington County, at least for a day. That number easily would outstrip the population of the City of Washington then, which was 15,874, according to the 1990 U.S. Census.

Any day that you drive on Park Avenue in North Franklin Township - up the hill overlooking the city of Washington - you will pass the most densely populated area of Washington County.

Today, the resident population (if it can be called that) of the 151-year-old Washington Cemetery officially exceeded the total above-ground, living population of metropolitan Washington.

Left: Alex Avery, a fourth-grade student at Joe Walker Elementary School, looks for a veteran's gravesite to place an American flag at Washington Cemetery in May 2005.

That includes the city of Washington, East Washington Borough and those portions of Canton, North Franklin, South Strabane, South Franklin, Amwell and Chartiers townships, say, in roughly a five-mile radius of the statue of George Washington atop the Washington County Courthouse.

Beginning with the first interment there on Nov. 1, 1853, more than 44,000 people have been buried on its more than 250 acres of rolling hills and sweeping vales, lush trees and vegetation and manicured lawns and meadows. That was when Washington was not all that many years removed from when it was known as Bassettown, and before that Catfish Camp.

Washington Cemetery marked its sesquicentennial in May 2003 with a formal rededication ceremony at the Serenity Chapel Mausoleum.

As of April 2004, according to Paul Shiring, superintendent of Washington Cemetery since 1978, 44,076 burials have been held there in the 151 years since infant John Morgan Hayes, son of Morgan Hayes, then a resident of West Maiden Street, was laid to rest Nov. 1, 1853. On average, 250 people are buried there annually.

Shiring, only the seventh superintendent in the history of the cemetery (the last four before Shiring were all members of the Crosbie family who held the position of sexton or superintendent for 110 years, from 1868 to 1978), estimates that as many as 100 visitors a day come through the gates. That number, he said, quadruples in the weeks leading up to Memorial Day.

In 1865, the year the Civil War ended, the monument to that great, wrenching and defining war was dedicated on the top of the hill overlooking the Civil War veterans' section. Cavalry Capt. Hugh P. Boon, Co. B-1, WVCav., Medal of Honor recipient, is buried there.

In 1920, the cemetery built an all-granite Community Mausoleum containing 500 crypts for those whose preference was above-ground entombment. In 1988, to meet the increasing demand for above-ground entombment, Serenity Chapel Mausoleum containing 630 crypts was built, and in 1997, the Garden Mausoleum containing an additional 456 crypts opened.

In 1925, the cemetery's original receiving vault, also an all-granite structure, was built for the temporary holding of bodies when burials could not be made because of particularly inclement weather. The receiving vault was renovated in 1985, becoming the cemetery's first cremation chamber. The cemetery provides such services for 30 funeral homes and averages 225 cremations per year.

In 1940, the old gatehouse was razed and new administration offices and superintendent's quarters were built.

In 1999, the Washington County Vietnam Veterans Memorial was dedicated, and in 2003, a bronze statue sculpted and forged by Alan Cottrill was dedicated in the Garden of Angels.

Seven miles of paved roads wind through the cemetery. A carillon

Above: A monument was erected at the entrance of Washington Cemetery in 2001 to honor Hugh Patterson Boon, who received the Medal of Honor for heroism in the battle of Sailor's Creek, Va. Boon, under the command of Gen. George Custer, captured the rebel flag on April 6, 1865. Boon died in January 1908 and is buried in the cemetery.

bell system at Serenity Chapel chimes every 15 minutes throughout the day and on the half-hour plays patriotic music. There are three dedicated meditation areas. The cemetery employs seven full-time groundskeepers and maintenance workers, two

Above: Washington Cemetery entrance on Upper Ten Mile Plank Road, now Park Avenue, circa 1900. The woman in this illustration is Ida Bedillion Crosbie, wife of David Crosbie (who was born in the old Gate House at the entrance to the cemetery).

History on the Hill

office personnel, a gateman, the superintendent and assistant superintendent.

More than a graveyard, Washington Cemetery is the final resting place to many of the most important and influential people in this region's history. Soldiers, heroes, statesmen, judges, politicians, businessmen and women, clergy, craftsmen, laborers, farmers, shopkeepers, wives, widows, spinsters, children and elders alike - men and women from all walks of life - are buried there.

Lives are commemorated there and loved ones are remembered. Amid all the gravestones and markers, and the vaults and crypts and plantings, it is a perpetual record of the area's history as well as a place of sanctuary.

And, there are more people in repose there than there are outside looking in as they pass the gates on Park Avenue.

Above: View from the top of Washington Cemetery.

Left: The Vietnam Veterans Memorial in Washington Cemetery.

'State' of the Art

Published October 16, 2005
Memories linger of good times at
the State Theater in Washington

By Louis Florian

Mary Allison recalls the State Theater as a place of refuge on Saturdays during World War II, when all the potential boyfriends were away in uniform.

"I remember seeing 'Rebecca' and sitting in the balcony with a girlfriend," she said. "Our guys were in the war and we cried through the whole movie."

The war eventually ended, and the guys came home to become husbands and fathers. They returned to a Washington whose downtown was thriving, with four movie theaters within a couple of blocks of each other. There was the Court on West Chestnut Street; the Basle (now the Uptown Theatre) at Main and Chestnut, and two theaters operated by Warner Brothers Studio – the Washington and the State, which stood on opposite sides of North Main near Pine Avenue.

The State, on the west side of the street, was Washington's premier movie house. It had a spacious lobby and two staircases

---

Left: The projection room at the State Theater was off-limits to other employees.

that led to the balcony, where there were three seating areas. Bob Patten, who worked as an usher at the State in 1952 and '53, said the balcony was generally used only on weekends unless there was a really big movie playing. One of the challenges ushers faced was watching for young couples who would try to sneak into the balcony when it wasn't open.

The building that housed the State was built in 1921 by a company organized by Spero Cosmus, who operated the Olympia Grill. The group opened the Capitol Theater, which local historian Ray Knestrick described as "the finest theater that Washington has enjoyed." The Harris Amusement Co. of Pittsburgh later bought the Capitol and changed the name to the State. "In 1932," Knestrick wrote, "a fire gutted the theater and it was remodeled and opened as a first-class motion picture house."

Cosmus, whose establishment was next door, continued to have an interest in the State even though he no longer owned it. Well into the 1950s, there was an entrance off the lobby into the Olympia, where one of the specialties was "the world on a stick" – ice cream in the shape of a globe. Patrons could buy popcorn and, later, candy bars, in the lobby of the State, but were forbidden to take them into the theater.

George Silvers and Jim Scott, who worked as ushers at the State in the early 1940s, recalled the manager, Herbert Allbright, who was an old vaudevillian from New York and drove one of the few Cadillacs in Washington.

"Before he went into the theater, he was a dealer in Las Vegas. He could pick up a stack of coins and tell you how many dollars were there," Scott said. Scott described Allbright's wife as "an elegant lady who was a former show girl." On particularly busy nights at the theater, Allbright would call for a police escort to take Mrs. Allbright home.

And some nights were particularly busy. Scott remembers Louis Armstrong and the Ink Spots playing at the State, and Tex Ritter once gave a show there. While live entertainment at a movie house is rare today, the State did it to compete with the Basle, which started the practice.

Every Thursday was Bank Night, when they gave away $50 in a drawing. There were double features twice a week on slow nights.

On holidays, the State had midnight shows.

Right: In 1960, the Klick family, from left, Martin, 3, dad Walter, mom Ruth, Michael, 10, and Pat, 15, buys tickets for a show at the State Theater on Main Street in Washington.

122

'State' of the Art

Silvers said the ushers had to get everybody out by 11 p.m.—there were always a few hangers-on who had to be chased out—and then they had to change the marquees for the midnight show, a particularly unpleasant job on cold nights.

The Friday before Labor Day in 1955, the regular feature was "Mister Roberts," but the State's ad in the Washington Observer announced a "Midnite Show Tonite"—Gene Kelly, Dan Dailey and Cyd Charisse in "It's Always Fair Weather."

A variation on this practice was "Bargain Nite," when you could come as late as 9 p.m. for the regular feature and then get a second movie for no additional price. The last night of "It's Always Fair Weather," for example, was followed by "The Man from Laramie," with James Stewart, which continued for the next few days.

Occasionally, the State would offer a "Giant cartoon circus," which the ads described as "17 cartoons and 2 hours of fun."

Patten, who left Washington in 1953 to join the Navy and now lives in Jacksonville, Fla., said becoming a movie usher was a way "to have some extra money in our pockets." He thinks he made 20 or 25 cents an hour.

"We had to learn the tricks of sneaking in so we could catch the kids who tried it," he said. "One kid would go in the theater and tell the usher he was looking for somebody. Then he would go to the side exit and open the door for other kids to come

Right: The State's marquee was a familiar sight when Washington's downtown was thriving.

in. They would leave one kid there to hold the door while the first one went back and told the usher he couldn't find the guy he was looking for. Then, he would go out the front door and over to the side door to get in."

On Friday afternoons, they would get kids playing hookey from school. Silver said the truant officer from Washington High School would come regularly to check the theater for students skipping class.

But as the '50s wore on, times got tougher for movie theaters because people could get the same kind of entertainment from television without leaving their homes and without paying an admission charge. The State was the first of the three Main Street theaters to close.

Nobody is even sure exactly when that happened. The Washington city directory for 1959-60 still lists the State at 63 N. Main, but the 1961 directory said the address was vacant. The State's lobby later became a drugstore and is now a game room.

Above: State Theater manager Michael Cardone works in his office in 1956.

Left: This photo was taken during one of the special events at the theater.

Right: This photo was taken after the great Thanksgiving snowstorm on Nov. 24, 1950. The scene shows Main Street heading north toward Chestnut Street. The State Theater is on the left, the Washington Theater (later the Penn) on the right, and the Basle Theater (later the Midtown) at the northeast corner of Main and Chestnut.

Index